# HMH SCIENCE DIMENSIONS™
## ECOLOGY & THE ENVIRONMENT

## Module C

This Write-In Book belongs to

_____

Teacher/Room

_____

### Houghton Mifflin Harcourt™

# Consulting Authors

## Michael A. DiSpezio

*Global Educator*
North Falmouth,
Massachusetts

Michael DiSpezio has authored many HMH instructional programs for Science and Mathematics. He has also authored numerous trade books and multimedia programs on various topics and hosted dozens of studio and location broadcasts for various organizations in the United States and worldwide. Most recently, he has been working with educators to provide strategies for implementing the Next Generation Science Standards, particularly the Science and Engineering Practices, Crosscutting Concepts, and the use of Evidence Notebooks. To all his projects, he brings his extensive background in science, his expertise in classroom teaching at the elementary, middle, and high school levels, and his deep experience in producing interactive and engaging instructional materials.

## Marjorie Frank

*Science Writer and Content-Area Reading Specialist*
Brooklyn, New York

An educator and linguist by training, a writer and poet by nature, Marjorie Frank has authored and designed a generation of instructional materials in all subject areas, including past HMH Science programs. Her other credits include authoring science issues of an award-winning children's magazine, writing game-based digital assessments, developing blended learning materials for young children, and serving as instructional designer and coauthor of pioneering school-to-work software. In addition, she has served on the adjunct faculty of Hunter, Manhattan, and Brooklyn Colleges, teaching courses in science methods, literacy, and writing. For *HMH Science Dimensions™*, she has guided the development of our K–2 strands and our approach to making connections between NGSS and Common Core ELA/literacy standards.

Acknowledgments

Cover credits: (garden snail) ©Johan Swanepoel/Alamy; (poison dart frog) ©Dirk Ercken/Alamy.

Section Header Master Art: (human cells, illustration) ©Sebastian Kaulitzki/Science Photo Library/Corbis

Printed in the U.S.A.

ISBN   978-0-544-86096-4

6 7 8 9 10  0877   25 24 23 22 21 20 19 18 17

4500677995         A B C D E F G

## Michael R. Heithaus, PhD

*Dean, College of Arts, Sciences & Education Professor, Department of Biological Sciences*
Florida International University
Miami, Florida

Mike Heithaus joined the FIU Biology Department in 2003 and has served as Director of the Marine Sciences Program and Executive Director of the School of Environment, Arts, and Society, which brings together the natural and social sciences and humanities to develop solutions to today's environmental challenges. He now serves as Dean of the College of Arts, Sciences & Education. His research focuses on predator-prey interactions and the ecological importance of large marine species. He has helped to guide the development of Life Science content in *HMH Science Dimensions™*, with a focus on strategies for teaching challenging content as well as the science and engineering practices of analyzing data and using computational thinking.

## Cary I. Sneider, PhD

*Associate Research Professor*
Portland State University
Portland, Oregon

While studying astrophysics at Harvard, Cary Sneider volunteered to teach in an Upward Bound program and discovered his real calling as a science teacher. After teaching middle and high school science in Maine, California, Costa Rica, and Micronesia, he settled for nearly three decades at Lawrence Hall of Science in Berkeley, California, where he developed skills in curriculum development and teacher education. Over his career, Cary directed more than 20 federal, state, and foundation grant projects and was a writing team leader for the Next Generation Science Standards. He has been instrumental in ensuring *HMH Science Dimensions™* meets the high expectations of the NGSS and provides an effective three-dimensional learning experience for all students.

# Program Advisors

**Paul D. Asimow, PhD**
*Eleanor and John R. McMillan Professor of Geology and Geochemistry*
California Institute of Technology
Pasadena, California

**Joanne Bourgeois**
*Professor Emerita*
*Earth & Space Sciences*
University of Washington
Seattle, WA

**Dr. Eileen Cashman**
*Professor*
Humboldt State University
Arcata, California

**Elizabeth A. De Stasio, PhD**
*Raymond J. Herzog Professor of Science*
Lawrence University
Appleton, Wisconsin

**Perry Donham, PhD**
*Lecturer*
Boston University
Boston, Massachusetts

**Shila Garg, PhD**
*Emerita Professor of Physics*
*Former Dean of Faculty & Provost*
The College of Wooster
Wooster, Ohio

**Tatiana A. Krivosheev, PhD**
*Professor of Physics*
Clayton State University
Morrow, Georgia

**Mark B. Moldwin, PhD**
*Professor of Space Sciences and Engineering*
University of Michigan
Ann Arbor, Michigan

**Ross H. Nehm**
Stony Brook University (SUNY)
Stony Brook, NY

**Kelly Y. Neiles, PhD**
*Assistant Professor of Chemistry*
St. Mary's College of Maryland
St. Mary's City, Maryland

**John Nielsen-Gammon, PhD**
*Regents Professor*
*Department of Atmospheric Sciences*
Texas A&M University
College Station, Texas

**Dr. Sten Odenwald**
*Astronomer*
NASA Goddard Spaceflight Center
Greenbelt, Maryland

**Bruce W. Schafer**
*Executive Director*
Oregon Robotics Tournament & Outreach Program
Beaverton, Oregon

**Barry A. Van Deman**
*President and CEO*
Museum of Life and Science
Durham, North Carolina

**Kim Withers, PhD**
*Assistant Professor*
Texas A&M University-Corpus Christi
Corpus Christi, Texas

**Adam D. Woods, PhD**
*Professor*
California State University, Fullerton
Fullerton, California

# Classic Reviewers

**Cynthia Book, PhD**
John Barrett Middle School
Carmichael, California

**Katherine Carter, MEd**
Fremont Unified School District
Fremont, California

**Theresa Hollenbeck, MEd**
Winston Churchill Middle School
Carmichael, California

**Kathryn S. King**
*Science and AVID Teacher*
Norwood Jr. High School
Sacramento, California

**Donna Lee**
*Science/STEM Teacher*
Junction Ave. K8
Livermore, California

**Rebecca S. Lewis**
*Science Teacher*
North Rockford Middle School
Rockford, Michigan

**Bryce McCourt**
*8th Grade Science Teacher/Middle*
*School Curriculum Chair*
Cudahy Middle School
Cudahy, Wisconsin

**Sarah Mrozinski**
*Teacher*
St. Sebastian School
Milwaukee, Wisconsin

**Raymond Pietersen**
*Science Program Specialist*
Elk Grove Unified School District
Elk Grove, California

## You are a scientist!
You are naturally curious.

# Have you ever wondered . . .

- why is it difficult to catch a fly?
- how a new island can appear in an ocean?
- how to design a great tree house?
- how a spacecraft can send messages across the solar system?

# HMH SCIENCE DIMENSIONS™

### will *SPARK* your curiosity!

## AND prepare you for

| | |
|---|---|
| ✓ | tomorrow |
| ✓ | next year |
| ✓ | college or career |
| ✓ | life! |

## Where do you see yourself in 15 years?

**Observe**

**Collect Data**

# Be a scientist.
### Work like real scientists work.

**Analyze**

# Be an engineer.
## Solve problems like engineers do.

**Define Problems**

**Test Solutions**

STEM

**Gather Information**

**Think Critically**

# Explain your world.
## Start by asking questions.

**Conduct Investigations**

Collaborate

Develop Explanations

Construct Arguments

# There's more than one way to the answer. What's YOURS?

# YOUR Program

**Write-In Book:**
- a brand-new and innovative textbook that will guide you through your next generation curriculum, including your hands-on lab program

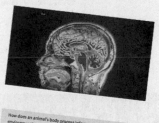

**Describing Information Processing in Animals**

Animals bodies gather and process information from their environment.

How does an animal's body process information from the environment?

Start typing...

**Interactive Online Student Edition:**
- a complete online version of your textbook enriched with videos, interactivities, animations, simulations, and room to enter data, draw, and store your work

**More tools are available online to help you practice and learn science, including:**
- Hands-On Labs
- Science and Engineering Practices Handbook
- Crosscutting Concepts Handbook
- English Language Arts Handbook
- Math Handbook

# Contents

## UNIT 1

# Matter and Energy in Living Systems

This kingfisher gets matter and energy from eating fish and other animals.

# Contents

## UNIT 2    65

# Relationships in Ecosystems

© Houghton Mifflin Harcourt • Image Credits: ©martin_hristov/Fotolia

Clown fish make their home within the stinging tentacles of sea anemone.
The clown fish is not harmed by the anemone, but potential predators can be.

# Contents

## UNIT 3

# Ecosystem Dynamics

Coral reefs have stunning biodiversity, but recover very slowly from disturbances.
They provide food, shelter coastlines from storms, and are sources of new medicines.

Whether you are in the lab or in the field, you are responsible for your own safety and the safety of others. To fulfill these responsibilities and avoid accidents, be aware of the safety of your classmates as well as your own safety at all times. Take your lab work and fieldwork seriously, and behave appropriately. Elements of safety to keep in mind are shown below and on the following pages.

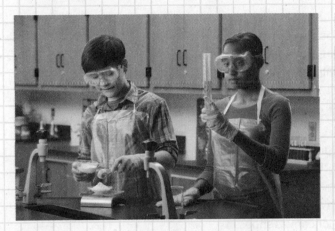

# Safety in the Lab

- ☐ Be sure you understand the materials, your procedure, and the safety rules before you start an investigation in the lab.

- ☐ Know where to find and how to use fire extinguishers, eyewash stations, shower stations, and emergency power shutoffs.

- ☐ Use proper safety equipment. Always wear personal protective equipment, such as eye protection and gloves, when setting up labs, during labs, and when cleaning up.

- ☐ Do not begin until your teacher has told you to start. Follow directions.

- ☐ Keep the lab neat and uncluttered. Clean up when you are finished. Report all spills to your teacher immediately. Watch for slip/fall and trip/fall hazards.

- ☐ If you or another student are injured in any way, tell your teacher immediately, even if the injury seems minor.

- ☐ Do not take any food or drink into the lab. Never take any chemicals out of the lab.

# Safety in the Field

- ☐ Be sure you understand the goal of your fieldwork and the proper way to carry out the investigation before you begin fieldwork.

- ☐ Use proper safety equipment and personal protective equipment, such as eye protection, that suits the terrain and the weather.

- ☐ Follow directions, including appropriate safety procedures as provided by your teacher.

- ☐ Do not approach or touch wild animals. Do not touch plants unless instructed by your teacher to do so. Leave natural areas as you found them.

- ☐ Stay with your group.

- ☐ Use proper accident procedures, and let your teacher know about a hazard in the environment or an accident immediately, even if the hazard or accident seems minor.

# Safety Symbols

To highlight specific types of precautions, the following symbols are used throughout the lab program. Remember that no matter what safety symbols you see within each lab, all safety rules should be followed at all times.

## Dress Code

- Wear safety goggles (or safety glasses as appropriate for the activity) at all times in the lab as directed. If chemicals get into your eye, flush your eyes immediately for a minimum of 15 minutes.
- Do not wear contact lenses in the lab.
- Do not look directly at the sun or any intense light source or laser.
- Wear appropriate protective non-latex gloves as directed.
- Wear an apron or lab coat at all times in the lab as directed.
- Tie back long hair, secure loose clothing, and remove loose jewelry. Remove acrylic nails when working with active flames.
- Do not wear open-toed shoes, sandals, or canvas shoes in the lab.

## Glassware and Sharp Object Safety

- Do not use chipped or cracked glassware.
- Use heat-resistant glassware for heating or storing hot materials.
- Notify your teacher immediately if a piece of glass breaks.
- Use extreme care when handling any sharp or pointed instruments.
- Do not cut an object while holding the object unsupported in your hands. Place the object on a suitable cutting surface, and always cut in a direction away from your body.

## Chemical Safety

- If a chemical gets on your skin, on your clothing, or in your eyes, rinse it immediately for a minimum of 15 minutes (using the shower, faucet, or eyewash station), and alert your teacher.
- Do not clean up spilled chemicals unless your teacher directs you to do so.
- Do not inhale any gas or vapor unless directed to do so by your teacher. If you are instructed to note the odor of a substance, wave the fumes toward your nose with your hand. This is called wafting. Never put your nose close to the source of the odor.
- Handle materials that emit vapors or gases in a well-ventilated area.
- Keep your hands away from your face while you are working on any activity.

## Safety Symbols, continued

### Electrical Safety

- Do not use equipment with frayed electrical cords or loose plugs.
- Do not use electrical equipment near water or when clothing or hands are wet.
- Hold the plug housing when you plug in or unplug equipment. Do not pull on the cord.
- Use only GFI-protected electrical receptacles.

### Heating and Fire Safety

- Be aware of any source of flames, sparks, or heat (such as flames, heating coils, or hot plates) before working with any flammable substances.
- Know the location of the lab's fire extinguisher and fire-safety blankets.
- Know your school's fire-evacuation routes.
- If your clothing catches on fire, walk to the lab shower to put out the fire. Do not run.
- Never leave a hot plate unattended while it is turned on or while it is cooling.
- Use tongs or appropriately insulated holders when handling heated objects.
- Allow all equipment to cool before storing it.

### Plant and Animal Safety

- Do not eat any part of a plant.
- Do not pick any wild plant unless your teacher instructs you to do so.
- Handle animals only as your teacher directs.
- Treat animals carefully and respectfully.
- Wash your hands throughly with soap and water after handling any plant or animal.

### Cleanup

- Clean all work surfaces and protective equipment as directed by your teacher.
- Dispose of hazardous materials or sharp objects only as directed by your teacher.
- Wash your hands throughly with soap and water before you leave the lab or after any activity.

# Student Safety Quiz

**Circle the letter of the BEST answer.**

1. Before starting an investigation or lab procedure, you should
   - **A.** try an experiment of your own
   - **B.** open all containers and packages
   - **C.** read all directions and make sure you understand them
   - **D.** handle all the equipment to become familiar with it

2. At the end of any activity you should
   - **A.** wash your hands thoroughly with soap and water before leaving the lab
   - **B.** cover your face with your hands
   - **C.** put on your safety goggles
   - **D.** leave hot plates switched on

3. If you get hurt or injured in any way, you should
   - **A.** tell your teacher immediately
   - **B.** find bandages or a first aid kit
   - **C.** go to your principal's office
   - **D.** get help after you finish the lab

4. If your glassware is chipped or broken, you should
   - **A.** use it only for solid materials
   - **B.** give it to your teacher for recycling or disposal
   - **C.** put it back into the storage cabinet
   - **D.** increase the damage so that it is obvious

5. If you have unused chemicals after finishing a procedure, you should
   - **A.** pour them down a sink or drain
   - **B.** mix them all together in a bucket
   - **C.** put them back into their original containers
   - **D.** dispose of them as directed by your teacher

6. If electrical equipment has a frayed cord, you should
   - **A.** unplug the equipment by pulling the cord
   - **B.** let the cord hang over the side of a counter or table
   - **C.** tell your teacher about the problem immediately
   - **D.** wrap tape around the cord to repair it

7. If you need to determine the odor of a chemical or a solution, you should
   - **A.** use your hand to bring fumes from the container to your nose
   - **B.** bring the container under your nose and inhale deeply
   - **C.** tell your teacher immediately
   - **D.** use odor-sensing equipment

8. When working with materials that might fly into the air and hurt someone's eye, you should wear
   - **A.** goggles
   - **B.** an apron
   - **C.** gloves
   - **D.** a hat

9. Before doing experiments involving a heat source, you should know the location of the
   - **A.** door
   - **B.** window
   - **C.** fire extinguisher
   - **D.** overhead lights

10. If you get chemicals in your eye you should
    - **A.** wash your hands immediately
    - **B.** put the lid back on the chemical container
    - **C.** wait to see if your eye becomes irritated
    - **D.** use the eyewash station right away, for a minimum of 15 minutes

*Go online to view the Lab Safety Handbook for additional information.*

# Matter and Energy in Living Systems

Giant pandas spend up to 16 hours each day eating up to 30 pounds of bamboo to provide them with energy.

The temperature on Mercury can vary between -280 °F and over 1,000 °F! That makes you think twice about complaining that it's too cold or too hot outside, doesn't it? Earth's distance from the sun provides Earth with a unique temperature range that supports life. Plant cells, such as those in bamboo, use light energy from the sun and materials from the environment to produce food for the plant. In turn, the matter and energy stored in plants provides food for animals, such as pandas. In this unit, you will investigate how matter and energy move through cells, organisms, and entire ecosystems.

# Why It Matters

Here are some questions to consider as you work through the unit. Can you answer any of the questions now? Revisit these questions at the end of the unit to apply what you discover.

| Questions | Notes |
|---|---|
| Where would you fit on a food web? | |
| How does the availability of fresh fruits and vegetables differ between seasons? How might these differences relate to the sun? | |
| When you eat food, how does your body use the energy and nutrients from the food? | |
| How do you feel after you eat foods high in sugar? Why do you think you feel this way? | |
| If homeowners received a composting bin along with their garbage and recycling bins, what impact could this have on the environment? | |

### Unit Starter: Analyzing the Flow of Matter and Energy

All animals, including humans, need to eat food to survive. Matter and energy move through an ecosystem as animals eat plants and other animals. Analyze the diagram to learn about "who eats whom" in this pond ecosystem.

The mosquito gets food from plants growing in the water and on land.

The dragonfly eats plants and mosquitoes.

The frog eats dragonflies and mosquitoes.

The snake eats the frog.

1. Number the organisms from 1 to 5 to represent the movement of matter and energy as one organism eats the next.

_____ mosquito

_____ snake

_____ dragonfly

_____ frog

_____ plants

Go online to download the Unit Project Worksheet to help you plan your project.

## Unit Project

## Food Webs around the World

Choose an ecosystem from any part of the world that interests you and research to find out what types of organisms live there. Make a food web to model the flow of energy and cycling of matter in this ecosystem, and identify a specific food chain to analyze closely.

# Matter and Energy in Organisms

This kingfisher gets matter and energy from eating fish and other animals.

**By the end of this lesson . . .**

you will be able to explain how organisms use matter and energy.

Go online to view the digital version of the Hands-On Lab for this lesson and to download additional lab resources.

# CAN YOU EXPLAIN IT?

**What happened to the matter and energy that were in these fruits when they were first picked?**

These fruits were once part of living plants. After they were picked they began to *decompose*, or break down. Eventually, a person looking at the space where these fruits lay will see no trace of them.

 Explore ONLINE!

**1.** Can you think of another example in which matter changes over time? How does your example compare or contrast with the example shown here?

 **EVIDENCE NOTEBOOK** As you explore this lesson, gather evidence to explain what happened to the matter and energy in the decomposed fruits.

# Describing Matter and Energy in Organisms

Over 250 million years ago, many species of plants and animals, including pine trees, dinosaurs, giant sea reptiles, and tiny mammals, lived on Earth. A mass extinction event 66 million years ago resulted in the loss of many species, including all dinosaurs and plesiosaurs. What happened to their bodies? Did they just disappear?

Plesiosaurs were giant sea reptiles that lived at the same time as dinosaurs.

2. **Discuss** Do you think that the materials that made up the bodies of plesiosaurs are still on Earth today?

## Matter in Organisms

The bodies of all living things are made of matter. **Matter** is anything—living or nonliving—that has mass and takes up space. A tree's leaves, trunk, and roots are made of matter. All the parts of your body are also made of matter. Even the tiniest organism, such as a single-celled bacterium, is made of matter.

Living things need matter to live because it provides them with the materials needed to grow and carry out life processes. For example, plants need water and air—both of which are matter—to make food. The food you eat and the air you breathe are made of matter. Without matter, living things would not be able to survive.

# Atoms Are the Building Blocks of Matter

Most of the matter in organisms is contained in cells, the smallest unit of living things. Cells are made of even smaller units called atoms. An *atom* is the smallest unit of a substance that maintains the properties of that substance. Nearly 100 types of atoms occur naturally on Earth. These types of atoms are called *elements*. Elements are the most basic substances on Earth. Oxygen and hydrogen are examples of elements. Different types of atoms can combine to form *compounds*. For example, if you combine oxygen and hydrogen together in the right proportions, water is formed.

## Elements of the Human Body, by Mass

**Oxygen 65.0%** Oxygen atoms help form water in the body. Water is 70% of the body's mass.

**Carbon 18.5%** Carbon atoms are the building blocks of many important molecules in the body.

**Hydrogen 9.5%** Hydrogen atoms help form water in the body and are important in the release of energy for the body.

**Nitrogen 3.3%** Nitrogen atoms are part of DNA and the amino acids that form proteins in the body.

**Calcium 1.5%** Calcium atoms are important for strong bones and teeth.

**Phosphorus 1.0%** Phosphorus works closely with calcium to build strong bones and teeth. It is also important for cell growth and repair.

**Other elements 1.2%** The 19 other elements have important functions in the body.

3. Which element makes up most of the mass of the human body? Explain why you think the body is made of a large percentage of this element.

# Atoms Bond to Form Molecules

A **molecule** is made up of two or more atoms held together by chemical bonds. The chemical bonds in molecules store energy. Cells and the substances they produce are made of molecules. Organisms need many different kinds of molecules for life processes. For example, the energy stored in the bonds of food molecules supplies the energy that cells and organisms need to stay alive.

Some molecules are very simple. For example, two hydrogen atoms and one oxygen atom form a water molecule. Water makes up about 70% of an organism. Most of the remaining 30% is made of very large molecules that contain hydrogen, carbon, and other elements. Organisms make some of these large molecules, but they must get the atoms from matter taken in from their environment.

**4.** In the molecules shown, color the hydrogen (H) atoms blue, the oxygen (O) atoms green, and the carbon (C) atoms red.

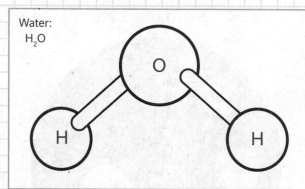

Water:
$H_2O$

Water can make up about 70% of an organism.

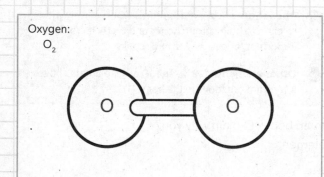

Oxygen:
$O_2$

Oxygen is used by cells to extract energy from food.

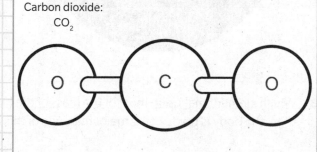

Carbon dioxide:
$CO_2$

Plants use carbon dioxide, water, and sunlight to make food.

**5.** How many carbon, hydrogen, and oxygen atoms are in the glucose molecule shown here?

_____ carbon

_____ hydrogen

_____ oxygen

Glucose is a sugar molecule used as a main source of energy for many cells.

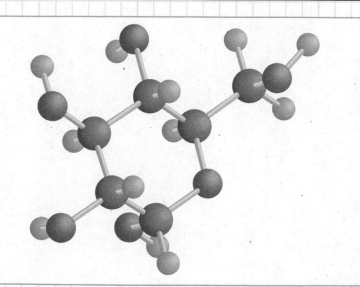

## Do the Math
# Analyze Size and Scale of Matter

Measuring between 4 and 6 meters tall, giraffes are the tallest mammals on Earth. They prefer to eat leaves and buds from trees but will also eat grasses, flowers, and fruits.

Giraffes get much of their water from eating acacia leaves. They can eat as much as 65 kilograms (about 140 pounds) of leaves each day!

6. Which choice below shows the matter that makes up the giraffe in order from smallest to greatest?

   **A.** atoms → molecules → cells → giraffe

   **B.** atoms → cells → molecules → giraffe

   **C.** cells → atoms → molecules → giraffe

7. Giraffes can weigh 1,300 kilograms (kg) or more. If they eat 65 kg of food each day, what percentage of their body weight do they consume in food each day?

# Energy in Organisms

Organisms need a constant source of energy to live, grow, and reproduce. **Energy** is the ability to cause change. Energy comes in many forms, including light energy from the sun and energy stored in the bonds of food molecules. When an organism eats food, the energy in the bonds of the food molecules becomes available to the organism for use in life processes. Some energy is stored for later use or converted to heat.

Different organisms get food in different ways. For example, plants depend on the sun's energy to make food molecules. Animals cannot make their own food, so they must get energy by eating plants or other animals.

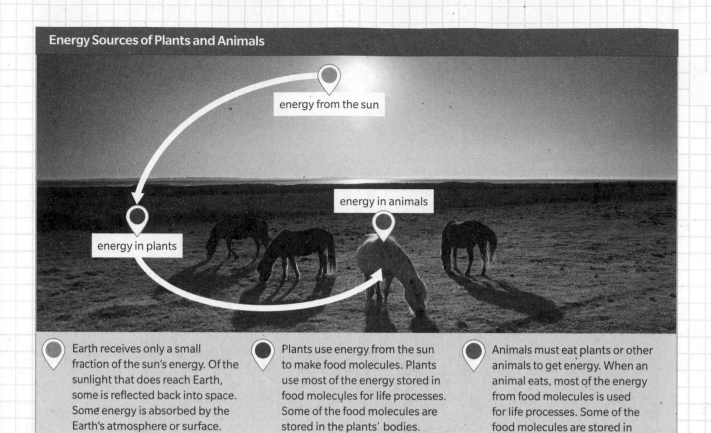

**Energy Sources of Plants and Animals**

energy from the sun

energy in animals

energy in plants

Earth receives only a small fraction of the sun's energy. Of the sunlight that does reach Earth, some is reflected back into space. Some energy is absorbed by the Earth's atmosphere or surface.

Plants use energy from the sun to make food molecules. Plants use most of the energy stored in food molecules for life processes. Some of the food molecules are stored in the plants' bodies.

Animals must eat plants or other animals to get energy. When an animal eats, most of the energy from food molecules is used for life processes. Some of the food molecules are stored in animals' bodies.

## Make an Analogy

Organisms need both matter and energy to perform functions. For example, organisms need matter and energy to move, keep their bodies warm, and control cell signaling and heart rhythms.

Other types of systems also need matter and energy to perform functions. For example, a car engine uses gasoline to produce the motion that makes the car move. Stoves and furnaces use natural gas to produce heat that cooks food and warms homes. Batteries use atoms to produce electricity that powers cell phones, computers, and flashlights.

8. Organisms get energy from the bonds that hold together food molecules. How do you think a car engine gets energy from gasoline?

_____

_____

_____

_____

9. Describe how the energy in gasoline changes form as it travels through a car engine. How does this compare to the way it changes form in an organism?

_____

_____

_____

_____

# Explaining How Organisms Obtain Matter and Energy

## Organisms Need Sources of Matter and Energy

Yikes! A young rabbit is nibbling on the lettuce that is growing in your garden. The lettuce is the rabbit's food. It provides the matter and energy that the rabbit needs to grow, move through your garden, chew your lettuce, and perform other tasks that keep the rabbit alive and healthy. Like the rabbit, all living organisms need a source of matter and energy.

10. **Discuss** Recall the foods you've eaten in the last few days. Think about whether each food came from a plant, an animal, or had a combination of ingredients. With a partner, record the food you ate in the correct column.

This apple is only one source of matter and energy for the girl.

| Plant | Animal |
|-------|--------|
|       |        |

11. Read about the organisms in the photos. Do you think they get their matter from the nonliving environment or from other organisms? Do you think they get their energy from the sun or other organisms? Record your answers.

| Image | Description | Answers |
|---|---|---|
| | These rhinos spend most of their time roaming through their environment to find plants to eat. | Matter:<br><br>Energy: |
| | When a tree falls in a forest, these fungi soon begin to live on its decaying trunk. | Matter:<br><br>Energy: |
| | Lianas are vines that climb tall trees so their leaves can reach the sunlight at the top of the canopy. | Matter:<br><br>Energy: |

## Producers

A **producer** is an organism that uses energy and matter from the environment to make its own food molecules. In order to live, producers must obtain energy and matter, such as carbon dioxide, water, and nutrients, from their environment.

Many producers, such as plants, algae, and some bacteria, use energy from sunlight to make sugar molecules from carbon dioxide and water. They use the sugar molecules as food. When producers break down the sugars they have made, and form new molecules, energy is released. This energy is used for life processes. Producers provide energy and matter for other living organisms that consume them.

The plants in this forest provide food for most of the other organisms that live there.

## Consumers

A **consumer** is an organism that gets energy and matter by eating other organisms. Humans and all other animals are consumers. Some consumers, such as rabbits, eat only plants. These consumers may eat any plant matter they can find. For example, elephants will eat grasses, bark, leaves, and fruit. Other consumers may specialize and eat only one part of a plant. Koalas eat only the leaves of eucalyptus trees, and pandas feed almost entirely on bamboo.

Not all consumers eat plants. Some consumers, such as spiders, frogs, and sharks, eat other animals. Other consumers have more variety in their diets. Animals such as ants, raccoons, and bears eat both plants and animals.

This lesser anteater's diet is mostly ants and termites.

## Decomposers

A **decomposer** is an organism that gets energy and matter by breaking down the remains of other organisms that have died. Decomposers also break down the wastes expelled by other organisms. Like consumers, decomposers use the bodies of other organisms as sources of matter and energy because they cannot make their own food. Fungi, such as mushrooms, often grow on dead tree trunks or in soil that is rich in decaying matter. Some bacteria, earthworms, and slugs are also decomposers.

Without decomposers, the matter that makes up organisms would not be recycled back to the nonliving environment. When decomposers break down remains and wastes, nutrients enter the soil and become available for use by other organisms. Decomposers also recycle matter into the air, such as carbon dioxide. Often, several different species of decomposers are involved in breaking down the dead organism.

Slugs process dead plant material and deposit the nutrients into the soil.

**EVIDENCE NOTEBOOK**

**12.** Which group of organisms is breaking down the matter and using the energy in the decaying fruit from the beginning of the lesson? Record your evidence.

# Investigate Decomposition

In this lab you will observe decomposition of plant matter in different soil types and explain how soil type affects the rate of decomposition.

The molecules that make up these compost materials are made of matter and stored energy.

## Procedure

**STEP 1** List factors that you think might affect the rate of decomposition.

### MATERIALS
- dry sand and potting soil
- graduated cylinder
- plastic baggies
- variety of fruits and vegetables, cut into pieces
- water

**STEP 2** Label three baggies for each condition (9 total): control, dry sand, and potting soil. Do not add soil to the control baggie. Add 1 cup dry sand and 1 cup potting soil to the corresponding baggies. To each baggie, add pieces of fruits and/or vegetables. The contents of each baggie should be identical, except for the type of soil.

**STEP 3** Use the graduated cylinder to add 100 mL of water to each baggie.

**STEP 4** Put the baggies into a cool, dark place, such as a closet or a drawer.

**STEP 5** For five days, at the same time each day, take the baggies out and observe them. Write your observations in the table. Note any variation observed between baggies within a condition.

| | Observations | | |
|---|---|---|---|
| Day | Control | Dry sand | Potting soil |
| 1 | | | |
| 2 | | | |
| 3 | | | |
| 4 | | | |
| 5 | | | |

## Analysis

**STEP 6** What are the differences in the soil types you used? How do you think these differences affect the rate of decomposition you observed?

**STEP 7** Explain how this activity is similar to and different from decomposition that takes place outdoors.

**STEP 8** What other factors could you test? Choose one of these factors and plan an experiment to test the relationship between that variable and decomposition. Perform your experiment, record your results, and construct a graph using your data to show the relationship between your variable and decomposition. Prepare a slide show presentation to share your results.

**Engineer It | Explore Bioremediation** Suppose that the next time you spill something, you could call on a swarm of microorganisms to clean up the mess. Bioremediation does just that. At a site where soil or water is contaminated by pollutants, scientists can use microorganisms, such as bacteria, to help break down the substance that is causing the problem. For example, oil spills contaminate soil and damage aquatic ecosystems. Not many organisms can decompose oil molecules because of their very stable, ringlike structure. But scientists have identified naturally occurring bacteria that can break down the oil molecules and use them as food. These bacteria convert the oil molecules into water and other nontoxic substances.

This bioremediation pit contains soil contaminated with crude oil. The successful culture of microbes that are able to break down the oil could clean this contaminated site.

13. Which of the following are constraints scientists need to consider when designing a bioremediation solution? Select all that apply.

    **A.** The maximum number of oil-digesting bacteria available.

    **B.** The temperature range in which the oil-digesting bacteria grow best.

    **C.** The cause of the oil contamination.

    **D.** Regulations about adding nonnative organisms to ecosystems.

14. Explain how using bioremediation to clean contaminated soil is similar to the process of decomposition in a natural environment.

## Explain the Need for "Plant Food"

15. You may have heard someone say they need to "feed" their plants. Products called *fertilizers* or *plant foods* are available for this purpose. A potted plant often grows better if it is given "plant food." Why does a potted plant need plant food if it is getting enough sunlight and water?

_____

_____

_____

_____

_____

_____

# Relating Cycling of Matter to Transfer of Energy

## Energy and Matter Are Conserved

How tall was the tallest tree you have ever seen? That tree was made of matter. Some trees can be more than 90 meters tall. That's a lot of matter! The tree also needed energy to grow. It did a lot of growing, so it needed a lot of energy.

Trees and other producers use the sun's energy to make food. Luckily, the sun is a nearly limitless source of energy for plants. Matter, however, is limited. The flow of energy drives the cycling of matter through different parts of the environment. Energy and matter cannot be created or destroyed.

A tree grows from a seed into a young sapling.

Over many years the sapling grows into a fully mature tree.

16. **Discuss** If matter cannot be created, then how does an organism grow and gain mass? With a partner, construct an explanation about how an organism grows if new matter is not created.

**EVIDENCE NOTEBOOK**

17. Could any of the matter and energy in the decaying fruits have disappeared? Record your evidence.

**18.** Draw a picture below each statement to show how matter is recycled and how energy flows in the life of a tree.

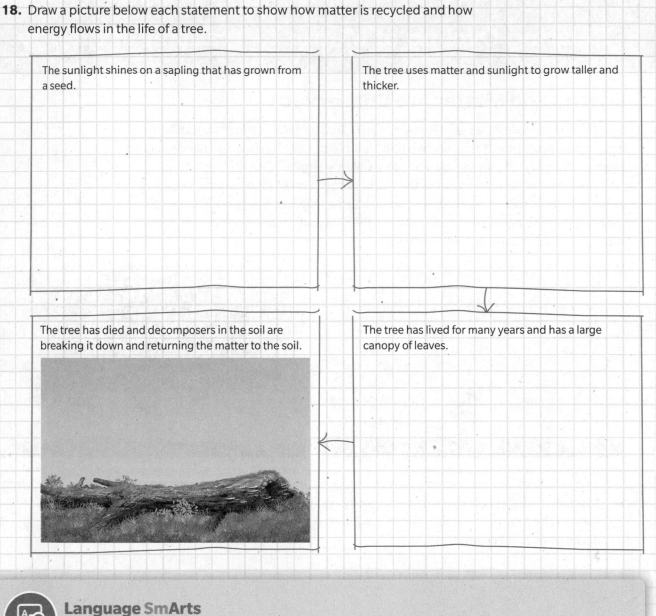

The sunlight shines on a sapling that has grown from a seed.

The tree uses matter and sunlight to grow taller and thicker.

The tree has died and decomposers in the soil are breaking it down and returning the matter to the soil.

The tree has lived for many years and has a large canopy of leaves.

**Language SmArts**

# Cite Evidence for Conservation of Matter and Energy

**19.** Use your drawings of the life of a tree to write a short explanatory text that explains how matter and energy were not created or destroyed over the course of the tree's life. Describe the flow of matter and energy in your explanation.

_____
_____
_____
_____
_____
_____
_____

# Continue Your Exploration

**Name:** _____  **Date:** _____

**Check out the path below or go online to choose one of the other paths shown.**

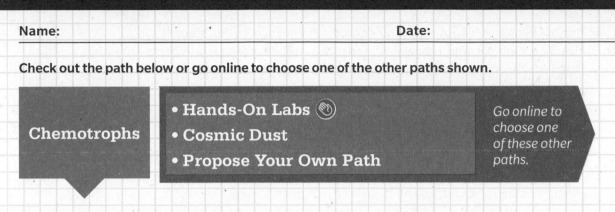

**Chemotrophs**

- **Hands-On Labs** 👆
- **Cosmic Dust**
- **Propose Your Own Path**

*Go online to choose one of these other paths.*

The sun is the source of almost all energy on Earth. *Phototrophs*—most plants, algae, and some bacteria—use energy from the sun to change water and carbon dioxide into sugars and oxygen. However, the sun is not the source of energy for organisms called *chemotrophs*. These organisms live in the deepest parts of the ocean, below 2,000 meters (6,562 feet). There it is completely dark and very cold. The sun's energy cannot reach these parts of the ocean.

On the ocean floor, extremely hot water gushes from below Earth's surface through hydrothermal vents. In the absence of sunlight, producers such as bacteria and other organisms living in and around these vents must find another source of energy to make their food. *Chemosynthesis* is the process by which carbon dioxide is converted to sugar molecules by using the energy stored in molecules, such as hydrogen sulfide. When bacteria break the bonds between atoms, and new bonds are formed, energy is released that can be used to make food, much like plants on the surface that use energy from the sun to make food.

The chemicals rising from this vent contain stored energy that some organisms can use.

# Continue Your Exploration

1. In addition to chemotrophs, a variety of other organisms live near hydrothermal vents, including shrimp, crabs, tubeworms, and octopuses. Choose the statements below that describe matter and energy in deep-sea vent ecosystems.

   A. Crabs are consumers that get matter and energy from eating other organisms that live near deep-sea vents.

   B. Chemotrophs get matter and energy from the molecules coming out of the sea floor.

   C. Chemotrophs get matter but not energy from the molecules coming out of the sea floor.

   D. Chemotrophs provide most of the matter and energy that is available to the other organisms that live near the deep-sea vent.

2. How are phototrophs and chemotrophs similar and different?

3. What would happen to chemotrophs if the sun suddenly stopped releasing energy? Would the chemotrophs survive? Why or why not?

4. **Collaborate** Conduct research with a classmate to learn more about chemotrophs. Find out about species of chemotrophs that have been discovered, as well as the technologies that help scientists explore deep-sea vents. Explore topics related to chemotrophs, such as the origin of life on Earth and the possibility of life on other planets.

# Can You Explain It?

**Name:** _____  **Date:** _____

**What happened to the matter and energy that were in these fruits when they were first picked?**

*Explore ONLINE!*

**EVIDENCE NOTEBOOK**

Refer to the notes in your Evidence Notebook to help you construct an explanation for what happened to the matter and energy in the fruits as they decomposed.

1. State your claim. Make sure your claim fully explains where the matter and energy went as the fruits decomposed.

2. Summarize the evidence you have gathered to support your claim and explain your reasoning.

# Checkpoints

**Answer the following questions to check your understanding of the lesson.**

**Use the photo to answer Questions 3 and 4.**

3. What happens to the food after the snail eats it? Select all that apply.

   **A.** The snail breaks apart the food molecules to get energy.

   **B.** The snail uses the matter in the food to grow.

   **C.** The snail uses the matter in the food to produce its own food.

   **D.** The snail uses energy from the sun to make food.

4. The plants in the photo get energy from the air / sun. The plants store the energy in the bonds / matter between atoms / cells that make up the food molecules. When the snail eats a plant, it uses the energy stored in bonds /atoms of the molecules to get energy. Matter is /is not destroyed in the process.

**Use the diagram to answer Question 5.**

5. Why do you think the starch molecule shown here is a good source of energy for an organism?

   **A.** The many bonds in the starch molecule store energy.

   **B.** The atoms in the starch molecule are made of matter.

   **C.** Starch is the only type of molecule that provides energy.

   **D.** A starch molecule is made of more than one kind of atom.

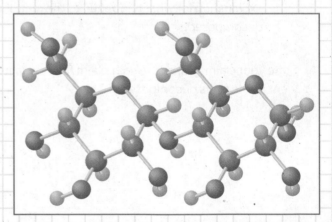

6. Number the sentences to show what will happen to an apple's matter and energy.

   _____ A deer eats the apple to get matter and energy.

   _____ The apple passes through the digestive system of the deer, returning some of the apple's matter and energy to the environment.

   _____ An apple tree uses the matter from the soil for life processes.

   _____ An apple falls from a tree and lands on the ground.

   _____ Decomposers break down the deer's waste to get matter and energy and return some matter to the soil.

# Interactive Review

**Complete this section to review the main concepts of the lesson.**

All living things need matter and energy to survive. Organisms get matter and energy from food.

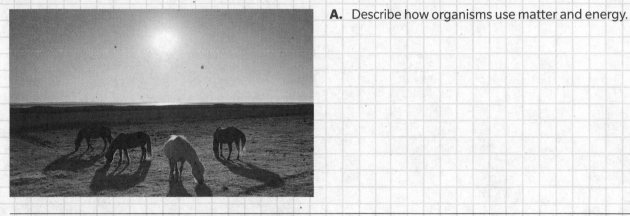

**A.** Describe how organisms use matter and energy.

Different types of organisms get matter and energy in different ways.

**B.** Make a table to compare and contrast how producers, consumers, and decomposers get matter and energy.

The transfer of energy drives the cycling of matter in organisms.

**C.** Make a labeled diagram that illustrates how the flow of energy drives the cycling of matter through organisms.

© Houghton Mifflin Harcourt • Image Credits: (t) ©mh-fotos/iStock/Getty Images Plus/ Getty Images; (m) ©Mikael Drackner/Moment/Getty Images

# Photosynthesis and Cellular Respiration

Underwater forests of kelp provide food and shelter for many species including fish, sea urchins, and sea lions.

**By the end of this lesson . . .**

you will be able to explain the roles of photosynthesis and cellular respiration in the flow of energy and matter through organisms.

## CAN YOU EXPLAIN IT?

### How can these microscopic organisms be so important for life on Earth?

Microscopic organisms called *phytoplankton* live near the sunlit surface of nearly all freshwater and saltwater environments.

1. Phytoplankton are a diverse group of unicellular organisms that are neither plants nor animals. Phytoplankton use sunlight, carbon dioxide, and nutrients to live and grow. Do you think phytoplankton are producers, consumers, or decomposers? Explain your reasoning.

**EVIDENCE NOTEBOOK** As you explore this lesson, gather evidence to explain why phytoplankton are so important for life on Earth.

# Analyzing the Chemistry of Cells

Did you know that chemical reactions are constantly happening in every cell of your body? Each cell performs many chemical reactions every second. During a chemical reaction, atoms are rearranged into different combinations. The new molecules formed by chemical reactions in cells are used as matter and energy for life processes.

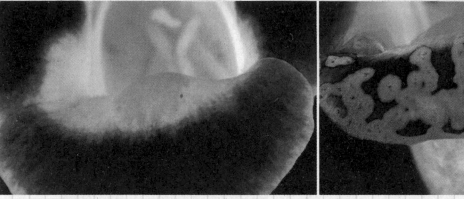

This flower has been placed in a chemical solution. A chemical reaction causes the color of the flower's petals to change from purple to yellow.

Explore
ONLINE!

2. These photos show the beginning and the end of a chemical reaction. What do you think happens to the atoms in the petals during this chemical reaction?

## Chemical Reactions

A **chemical reaction** is a process in which atoms are rearranged to produce new substances. The starting substances in a chemical reaction are called *reactants*. The substances formed in a chemical reaction are called *products*. During a chemical reaction, bonds that hold atoms together may be broken or formed. An energy input is needed to break the bonds between atoms, and energy is released when new bonds are formed. Neither matter nor energy is created or destroyed during a chemical reaction.

Many different chemical reactions take place in living systems. For example, the production of food molecules in the cells of producers involves chemical reactions. The cells of all organisms use chemical reactions to release energy from food molecules.

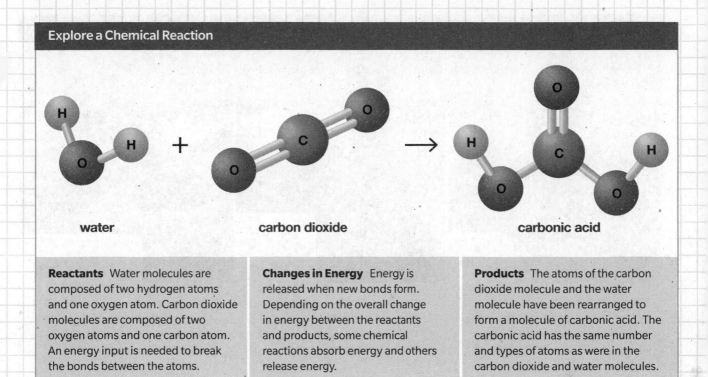

## Explore a Chemical Reaction

water + carbon dioxide → carbonic acid

**Reactants** Water molecules are composed of two hydrogen atoms and one oxygen atom. Carbon dioxide molecules are composed of two oxygen atoms and one carbon atom. An energy input is needed to break the bonds between the atoms.

**Changes in Energy** Energy is released when new bonds form. Depending on the overall change in energy between the reactants and products, some chemical reactions absorb energy and others release energy.

**Products** The atoms of the carbon dioxide molecule and the water molecule have been rearranged to form a molecule of carbonic acid. The carbonic acid has the same number and types of atoms as were in the carbon dioxide and water molecules.

## Chemical Equations

A chemical reaction can be modeled by writing a chemical equation, which uses symbols to show the relationship between the starting materials and the materials produced in the reaction. Each type of atom, or element, is indicated by its symbol.

3. Complete the chemical equation by filling in the molecules and symbols. Use the model above to help you.

☐ ☐ ☐ ☐ ☐

**WORD BANK**
- $CO_2$   • +
- $H_2O$   • →
- $CH_2O_3$

4. The molecular model in the image and the chemical equation above both model the same chemical reaction. Compare and contrast these two models.

## Carbon-Based Molecules in Cells

Carbon-based molecules are the building blocks of living things. The unique structure of a carbon atom allows it to form bonds with other carbon atoms or with different atoms, such as hydrogen, oxygen, and nitrogen. The sugar and fat molecules that provide energy to cells are made up of carbon, hydrogen, and oxygen atoms. Nucleic acids that give the instructions to make proteins, as well as the amino acids that form proteins, are also carbon-based molecules. All animal and plant cells are powered by energy that comes from carbon-based molecules.

## Molecular Structure of Foods

Several types of carbon-based molecules can provide energy for cells. Most producers use energy from sunlight to make food molecules. Consumers, including people, must eat other living things to get food molecules.

Sweet potato plants store starches, a type of carbohydrate, in specialized roots. Carbohydrates are an important source of energy and materials used to build cell parts.

Salmon flesh is high in protein. Proteins are responsible for most of the work performed in cells, including transport, growth, and repair.

The fruit of an avocado plant is high in fat, which is a type of lipid. Lipids are a rich source of energy in the form of stored reserves.

5. How does chemical energy become available to the cells of consumers? Number the statements to show the sequence of events.

_____ Consumers eat food to get carbon-based food molecules.

_____ Producers capture energy from the sun to produce sugars.

_____ Chemical reactions release the energy stored in carbon-based food molecules.

_____ Energy from the sun powers chemical reactions that produce carbon-based sugar molecules.

## Model a Chemical Reaction

6. The equation that represents the chemical reaction shown is $CH_4 + 2O_2 \rightarrow CO_2 + 2H_2O$. Which molecules are the reactants? Which molecules are the products?

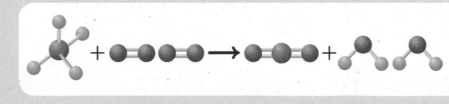

_____

_____

_____

7. What does the equation tell you about the number of atoms of each kind in the original molecules and the new molecules?

_____

_____

_____

# Investigating Photosynthesis

What did you eat for breakfast this morning? Maybe you had scrambled eggs and some toast. These breakfast foods help to provide the cells of your body with the energy they need.

Producers, such as plants and algae, don't "eat" their food. Most producers use energy from sunlight to make food out of carbon dioxide and water. The energy from sunlight powers chemical reactions that produce carbon-based food molecules.

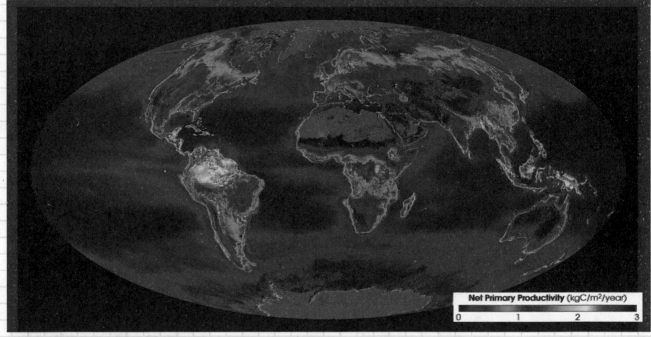

Net Primary Productivity (kgC/m²/year)

0    1    2    3

*Primary productivity* is a measure of the rate of conversion of the sun's energy into matter by the producers in an ecosystem.

8. **Discuss** With a partner, discuss the patterns you see in the map. Why do you think primary productivity is important for the health of an ecosystem?

 **EVIDENCE NOTEBOOK**

9. Identify areas on the map where phytoplankton might be the main producers. How much primary productivity is found in areas where phytoplankton are abundant? Record your evidence.

**Hands-On Lab**

# Investigate the Effect of Sunlight on *Elodea*

You will observe an aquatic plant, *Elodea*, to determine the relationship between sunlight and carbon dioxide uptake by the plant.

## Procedure

**STEP 1** Based on your understanding of how producers make food, make a prediction about the relationship between sunlight and carbon dioxide uptake by a plant.

**STEP 2** Bromothymol blue is an indicator dye that turns yellow when carbon dioxide and water react to form an acid. Prepare the bromothymol blue solution by measuring 150 mL of water into the graduated cylinder. Pour the water into a flask and add 20–25 drops of bromothymol blue. Swirl gently to mix. Observe and describe the color of the solution.

**STEP 3** Label three large test tubes for each parameter: control, wrapped, and unwrapped. Cover "wrapped" tubes in foil, making sure that light cannot reach inside of the tube.

**STEP 4** Use a straw to gently blow carbon dioxide from your lungs into the flask. Stop immediately when you see the color change to yellow. Use extreme caution to be sure not to inhale the solution through the straw. Notify your teacher immediately if you accidentally do so.

**STEP 5** Fill each tube about halfway with the solution. Clean up any spills on the table or floor immediately. Place a piece of *Elodea* into each of the wrapped and unwrapped tubes. Do not place *Elodea* in the control tubes. Top off the tubes with solution to be sure the *Elodea* is completely submerged. Cap all three tubes tightly. Be sure to wash your hands thoroughly.

**STEP 6** Describe the importance of having one tube that does not contain *Elodea*.

This *Elodea* plant is in a solution of water and bromothymol blue.

**STEP 7** Place the tubes in a beaker or tube rack and position them near a window or light source. Allow the tubes to sit in the light for as many as 24 hours. Record your observations in the data table.

| Observations | | | | | |
|---|---|---|---|---|---|
| Control | | Unwrapped | | Wrapped | |
| Start | 24 h | Start | 24 h | Start | 24 h |
| | | | | | |

## Analysis

**STEP 8** What do you observe about the three tubes? Do they look the same or different? Why or why not?

**STEP 9** Explain whether or not your data support your prediction.

**STEP 10** What do your observations tell you about the effect of sunlight on plants? Use your observations of the three tubes to provide evidence for your argument.

© Houghton Mifflin Harcourt

# Photosynthesis

**Photosynthesis** is a series of chemical reactions in which the cells of producers—including plants, algae, and some bacteria—use energy from the sun to make carbon-based food molecules, called *sugars*. In these reactions, carbon dioxide and water combine to form sugar molecules and release oxygen. Chemical energy is released when the sugar molecules are broken down and their atoms are used to form new products. The sugars can be used by the plant immediately for life processes, or they can be stored for later use. The oxygen is released into the atmosphere.

*Explore ONLINE!*

Streaming of the cytoplasm in *Elodea* cells allows the chloroplasts to move around the cell in response to light.

## Explore Photosynthesis

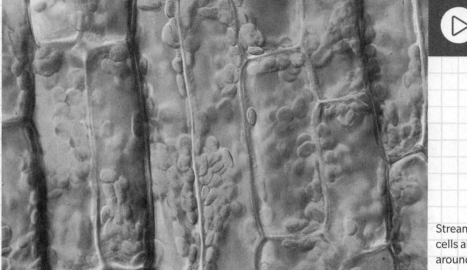

water

carbon dioxide

chloroplast

oxygen

sugar

**Reactants** The starting materials of photosynthesis are carbon dioxide ($CO_2$), water ($H_2O$), and light energy from the sun.

**Changes in Energy** Photosynthesis takes place inside organelles called *chloroplasts*. These reactions absorb, or store, energy.

**Products** The products of photosynthesis are oxygen ($O_2$) and sugar molecules ($C_6H_{12}O_6$). The sugar molecules will be used to make energy for the cell.

## Capturing Light Energy

Photosynthesis needs an input of light energy. Cell structures called *chloroplasts* capture light energy from the sun. Chloroplasts are only found in the cells of plants and other producers that use photosynthesis. Photosynthesis takes place in the chloroplasts.

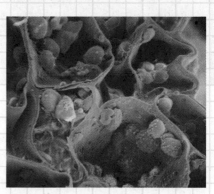

This scanning electron micrograph (SEM) of the cut edge of a leaf shows the chloroplasts inside each of the cells.

## Storing Energy in Chemical Bonds

All chemical bonds are sources of energy. During photosynthesis, light energy is used to make sugar molecules. These molecules can be broken down and rearranged by cells to provide energy for life processes. In plants, the sugar that is not used is stored in the plant's body. It is often stored as starch in the plant's stem and roots, such as in the sweet potato you observed earlier in this lesson.

**WORD BANK**
- $6O_2$
- $6CO_2$
- $6H_2O$
- light energy
- $C_6H_{12}O_6$

10. Use the symbols in the Word Bank to complete the chemical equation for photosynthesis.

$$\boxed{\phantom{xxxxx}} + \boxed{\phantom{xxxxx}} + \boxed{\phantom{xxxxx}} \longrightarrow \boxed{\phantom{xxxxx}} + \boxed{\phantom{xxxxx}}$$

---

### Engineer It
# Explore Use of Algae as Biofuel

*Biofuels* are fuels that are produced from plant or animal matter. The gasoline we use to fuel our cars is ancient biofuel, or *fossil fuel*, because it is made from decomposed plants and animals that have been buried in the ground for millions of years. Because fossil fuels are not renewable and extracting them from the ground can harm the environment, scientists are looking for new sources of biofuel. Biofuel made from algae is one possibility.

Algae can be grown in freshwater, salt water, and even wastewater environments. Algae grow quickly, producing a large amount of energy-rich lipids that can be converted to fuel.

11. Which statements identify possible advantages of algal biofuel? Choose all that apply.
   A. Algae grow quickly and are a renewable source of energy.

   B. Algae can be grown in water sources that cannot be used for drinking or agriculture.

   C. Algal biofuel use is not established on a large scale, so farming and fuel production methods cannot meet current global needs for energy.

   D. Algae can be supplied with the carbon dioxide they need to grow using emissions from power plants and other sources.

# Describing Cellular Respiration

Think of the last time you tried to hold your breath. It's not easy! That's because you—like nearly all living things—need a constant supply of oxygen to live. Organisms get oxygen from their environment.

**12. Discuss** Why do you think living things need oxygen?

Oxygen can enter this frog's body through its skin.

## Cellular Respiration

The cells of all living things need energy, which they get from food. When cells break down food molecules, the energy stored in chemical bonds is released. **Cellular respiration** is a process that uses oxygen to release the energy stored in food molecules. Producers, consumers, and some other types of organisms use cellular respiration.

**Explore Cellular Respiration**

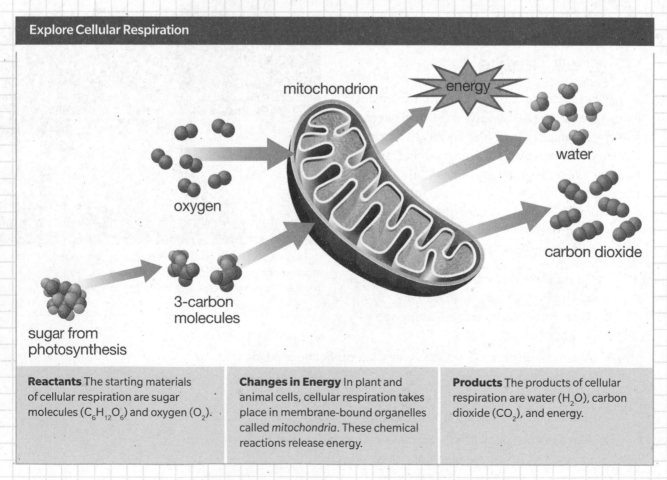

mitochondrion

energy

oxygen

water

sugar from photosynthesis

3-carbon molecules

carbon dioxide

**Reactants** The starting materials of cellular respiration are sugar molecules ($C_6H_{12}O_6$) and oxygen ($O_2$).

**Changes in Energy** In plant and animal cells, cellular respiration takes place in membrane-bound organelles called *mitochondria*. These chemical reactions release energy.

**Products** The products of cellular respiration are water ($H_2O$), carbon dioxide ($CO_2$), and energy.

## Using Oxygen

Cellular respiration occurs in several stages. In plant and animal cells, the first stage takes place in the cytoplasm, where each sugar molecule is broken down into smaller molecules. The next stages take place in the mitochondria. There, the smaller molecules are broken down even more. The chemical reactions that take place in the mitochondria require a lot of oxygen.

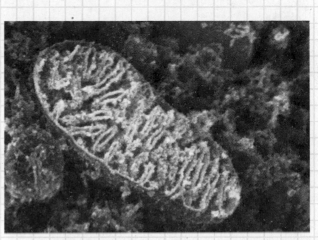

## Releasing Energy

Energy is released during all stages of cellular respiration. A small amount of energy is released when the sugar molecules are broken down in the cytoplasm. A large amount of energy is released by the chemical reactions in the mitochondria. Cells use this energy for life processes. The other products of cellular respiration—water and carbon dioxide—are released by the cell.

The many folds and compartments of the inner mitochondrial membrane increase the total surface area.

**13.** Use the symbols in the Word Bank to write the reactants and products in the correct places in the chemical equation for cellular respiration.

**WORD BANK**
- $6H_2O$
- $6CO_2$
- $6O_2$
- energy
- $C_6H_{12}O_6$

$$\boxed{\phantom{xxxx}} + \boxed{\phantom{xxxx}} \longrightarrow \boxed{\phantom{xxxx}} + \boxed{\phantom{xxxx}} + \boxed{\phantom{xxxx}}$$

### Do the Math
# Compare Reactants and Products

In a chemical reaction, bonds are broken and formed as atoms are rearranged to produce new substances. Find out whether any matter in the reactants is lost during a chemical reaction.

**14.** Count the number of each type of atom in the reactants and products of cellular respiration. Use the image and text about cellular respiration to help you.

| Type of atom | Number of atoms in reactants | Number of atoms in products |
|---|---|---|
| carbon (C) | | |
| hydrogen (H) | | |
| oxygen (O) | | |

**15.** What do your calculations tell you about the conservation of matter?

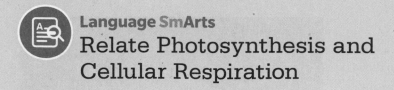

## Language SmArts
# Relate Photosynthesis and Cellular Respiration

**16.** Fill in the missing labels to complete the diagram.

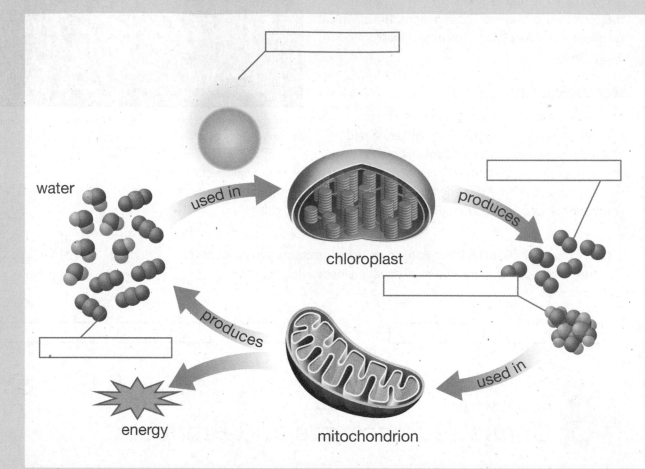

water    used in    chloroplast    produces

produces

energy    mitochondrion    used in

**17.** How are the starting reactants and the products of photosynthesis and cellular respiration related?

_____

_____

_____

_____

_____

_____

_____

_____

**EVIDENCE NOTEBOOK**

**18.** How do other organisms use the products of photosynthesis from phytoplankton? Record your evidence.

© Houghton Mifflin Harcourt

# Continue Your Exploration

Name: _____  Date: _____

**Check out the path below or go online to choose one of the other paths shown.**

**Fermentation**

- **Hands-On Lab** 🖐
- **Primary Productivity**
- **Propose Your Own Path**

*Go online to choose one of these other paths*

When there isn't enough oxygen available for cellular respiration, organisms can release energy from sugars through a process called *fermentation*. Like cellular respiration, fermentation releases energy that cells can use. However, it does not require oxygen, and it does not release as much energy as cellular respiration. There are two main types of fermentation: lactic acid fermentation and alcoholic fermentation.

Think about the last time you exercised so hard that your muscles became sore. That soreness is evidence of *lactic acid fermentation*. When your muscle cells run out of oxygen, they use this type of fermentation to release more energy. Lactic acid fermentation also produces carbon dioxide and lactic acid. The buildup of lactic acid causes muscles to feel weak and sore. Some types of bacteria also use lactic acid fermentation. Yogurt and cheese are made by adding these types of bacteria to milk. The buildup of lactic acid thickens the milk, eventually turning it into cheese.

Many yeasts, which are single-celled fungi, use *alcoholic fermentation* to release energy. Carbon dioxide and alcohol are also produced in this process. Alcoholic fermentation is important to bakers because the carbon dioxide produced by yeast creates air pockets in bread dough, causing it to rise.

Cheese is a food that is made by lactic acid fermentation.

When you perform rapid, vigorous exercise, fermentation releases energy in your muscles.

# Continue Your Exploration

1. Ethanol is a biofuel made from corn. The corn is ground and water is added. The substance goes through several more steps before yeast is added, and the sugars in it are converted to ethanol and carbon dioxide. What process is part of the making of this biofuel?

   **A.** cellular respiration

   **B.** alcoholic fermentation

   **C.** lactic acid fermentation

2. How are cellular respiration and fermentation similar and different?

3. Some bakers of sourdough and a few other types of bread have what they call "starter dough." This dough contains yeast from which they make all their bread. Some starter dough is more than 100 years old. The dough has to be "fed" more flour and water on a regular basis for it to remain usable. Why must the starter dough be "fed"?

4. **Collaborate** Discuss with a classmate that even though fermentation is necessary when our muscles cannot get enough oxygen, it causes a sore feeling in the muscles. Research lactic acid fermentation in the body to find out the physiological reason for muscle soreness. Prepare a multimedia presentation to share your findings.

# Can You Explain It?

**Name:** _____  **Date:** _____

How can these microscopic organisms be so important for life on Earth?

**EVIDENCE NOTEBOOK**

Refer to the notes in your Evidence Notebook to help you construct an explanation for why phytoplankton are so important for life on Earth.

**1.** State your claim. Make sure your claim fully explains why phytoplankton are so important for life on Earth.

**2.** Summarize the evidence you have gathered to support your claim and explain your reasoning.

# Checkpoints

Answer the following questions to check your understanding of the lesson.

Use the photo to answer Questions 3–4.

3. Which of the statements below are true? Select all that apply.

A. The tree uses photosynthesis to get energy from food molecules; the elephant uses cellular respiration to get energy from food molecules.

B. The tree and the elephant both use cellular respiration to get energy from food molecules.

C. Sunlight is the ultimate source of energy for both the tree and the elephant.

D. The tree and the elephant both use photosynthesis to make food molecules.

4. The tree produces oxygen / carbon dioxide as a product of photosynthesis / cellular respiration. The elephant and the tree take in the oxygen / carbon dioxide and use it to break down sugars / energy through the process of photosynthesis / cellular respiration.

---

Use the equations to answer Question 5.

5. Which of the statements are true about the two chemical reactions? Select all that apply.

A. Equation A summarizes photosynthesis, and Equation B summarizes cellular respiration.

B. Equation A summarizes cellular respiration, and Equation B summarizes photosynthesis.

C. Both chemical reactions produce oxygen and energy.

D. The products of Equation A are the starting materials for Equation B.

> **Equation A:**
> $6CO_2 + 6H_2O + energy \rightarrow C_6H_{12}O_6 + 6O_2$
>
> **Equation B:**
> $C_6H_{12}O_6 + 6O_2 \rightarrow 6CO_2 + 6H_2O + energy$

6. Animals that eat only meat, such as dolphins, do not get much sugar (carbohydrate) from their diets. Choose the statement below that best explains how a dolphin gets the energy it needs from its food.

A. The dolphin does not use cellular respiration to get energy from food.

B. The dolphin is not very active so it does not need a lot of energy to function.

C. The dolphin's body is able to break down other carbon-based molecules, such as proteins and fats, to use as an energy source for cellular respiration.

D. The dolphin gets the energy it needs directly from sunlight.

# Interactive Review

**Complete this section to review the main concepts of the lesson.**

Chemical reactions provide the energy that cells need to perform functions.

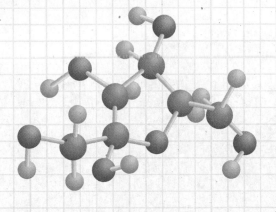

**A.** Explain how carbon-based molecules provide energy to cells.

Photosynthesis is a series of chemical reactions in which producers convert light energy from the sun to energy that is stored in the bonds of sugar molecules.

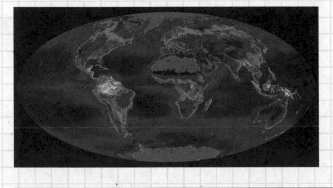

**B.** Create a diagram that models photosynthesis.

Cellular respiration is a process that uses oxygen to release energy stored in food molecules.

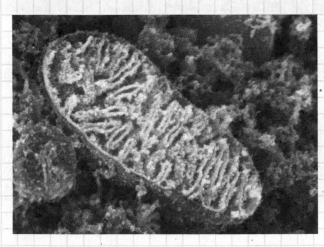

**C.** Create a diagram that models cellular respiration.

# Matter and Energy in Ecosystems

This wetland ecosystem supports a large community of plants, birds, fish, and other animals.

**By the end of this lesson . . .**

you will be able to explain how the flow of energy drives the cycling of matter in ecosystems.

© Houghton Mifflin Harcourt • Image Credits: ©Yannick Molgne/EyeEm/Getty Images

# CAN YOU EXPLAIN IT?

**How could the reintroduction of wolves to Yellowstone have led to an increase in the beaver population?**

Beavers rely on trees for food and building materials, particularly during Yellowstone's snowy winters.

*Explore ONLINE!*

By 1926, after decades of targeted hunting, the last wolves were removed from Yellowstone National Park. The wolves were reintroduced to Yellowstone in 1995, causing a ripple of change through the park. Elk, coyotes, beavers, birds, and plant life were all affected by the reintroduction of Yellowstone's top predator.

1. Think about the resources that wolves and beavers in Yellowstone might share. Record at least three possible connections between wolves and beavers.

**EVIDENCE NOTEBOOK** As you explore the lesson, gather evidence to explain how the return of wolves caused Yellowstone's beaver population to increase.

© Houghton Mifflin Harcourt • Image Credits: ©©Gregory B Balvin/Image Bank Film/Getty Images

# Analyzing Energy Flow in Ecosystems

## Energy Transfer in Ecosystems

You might think of a pond as a quiet and peaceful place to enjoy nature. A pond may seem quiet, but many interactions are taking place at all times. Plants that live within and around the pond use energy from the sun to make food. Ducks, herons, and other birds visit the pond to bathe, nest, and feed on the plants and animals in and around the pond. Fish, dragonfly larvae, and frogs hunt prey in the shallow water. Raccoons prowl for a meal on the shore. Microbes and earthworms break down nonliving plant and animal matter. By doing so, they return nutrients to the muddy soil of the pond.

A pond, a desert, or a forest is an *ecosystem*, a complex organization of interdependent parts. Every ecosystem involves the flow of energy and cycling of nonliving resources through a web of producers, consumers, and decomposers.

2. Label the organisms in this pond ecosystem as a producer, consumer, or decomposer.

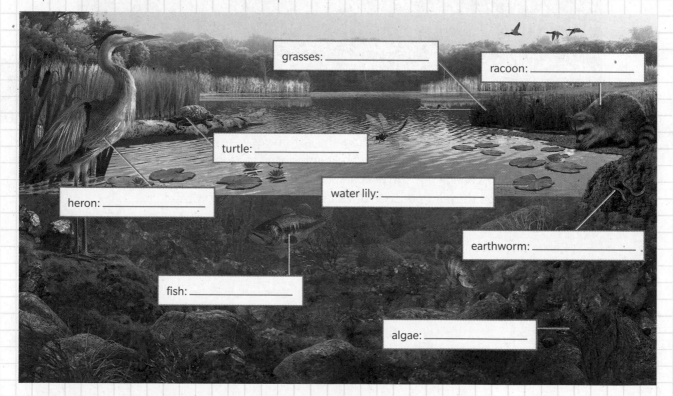

grasses: _____

racoon: _____

turtle: _____

water lily: _____

heron: _____

earthworm: _____

fish: _____

algae: _____

3. Only producers are able to capture energy from the sun and matter from the environment to make food. How does energy that comes from the sun get to every other organism in an ecosystem? How does matter from the environment enter every other organism?

## Food Chains

A *food chain* is a pathway that energy and nutrients can follow through an ecosystem. Producers make up the first level of a food chain. For example, the producers in a tropical rain forest include many species of grass, flowering ground plants, and fruit trees. Insects and other plant eaters get energy by eating these producers. Other consumers, such as lizards and birds, eat the insects. Large snakes and jaguars are at the top of the food chain. They hunt and eat lizards, birds, and smaller mammals that live in the rain forest. Decomposers complete the food chain. They break down nonliving plant and animal matter and return nutrients to the soil, where they can be used by producers.

### Construct a Food Chain

**4.** Draw a diagram that shows the organisms below arranged into a food chain. You can use organism names or drawings. Use arrows to show the flow of energy.

## Food Webs

Different types of animals may share food sources. In the tropical rain forest, grasshoppers, fruit bats, and relatives of rhinos called *tapirs* feed on plants. Monkeys, iguanas, and birds eat plants, grasshoppers, and butterflies. Jaguars eat iguanas, tapirs, and monkeys. These interconnected food chains are an example of a **food web,** a model that shows how energy flows between organisms in an ecosystem. The size of a food web depends on the nonliving resources available to producers in the ecosystem. Food web diversity depends on various factors. One factor is how predators control the population size of lower-level consumers.

Arrows in a food web diagram show the direction of energy flow, from where it is stored in a plant or animal to where it travels when that plant or animal is consumed. All energy paths begin at the producer level. Consumers feed on plants, animals, or both. Decomposers obtain energy by breaking down nonliving remains of organisms.

## Feeding Relationships in a Tropical Rain Forest

Explore this tropical rain forest food web. Identify one of the food chains that is shown with arrows. Trace this chain with your finger, starting with the producer. As you trace the chain, think about how matter and energy are flowing between living things at each step.

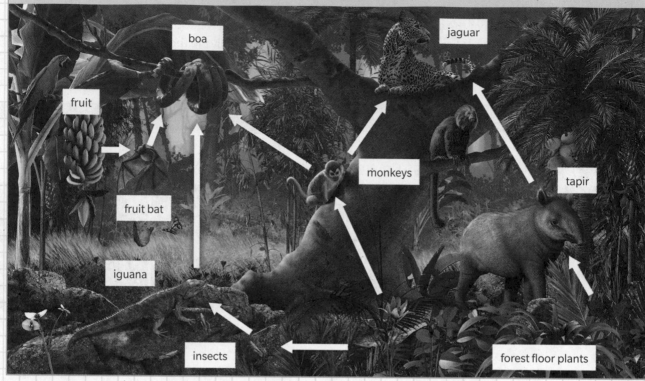

5. Identify two food chains that share at least one organism. Write each food chain below, showing the flow of energy with arrows.

6. If iguanas were removed from the ecosystem, the population of grasshoppers would most likely increase/decrease. The population of boas would most likely increase / decrease.

 **EVIDENCE NOTEBOOK**

   7. Beavers use plant material for food and building their homes. Elk and deer are also plant consumers in Yellowstone. How do you think the beavers, elk, deer, and wolves are related in a food web?

**Hands-On Lab**

# Model Energy Flow in an Ecosystem

You will model energy transfer in a meadow ecosystem. Use evidence from your model to explain why the ecosystem supports different numbers of organisms at different feeding levels.

## Procedure and Analysis

**STEP 1** On a table, lay out the sun card, all plant and rabbit cards, and the fox card. Place all bean packets around the sun.

**STEP 2** Model photosynthesis by placing one packet of beans from the sun on each grass card. Place 10 beans from each packet on top of each grass card to represent the energy stored in the grass. Set the rest of the beans aside to represent energy used by the grasses and transferred to the environment as heat.

**STEP 3** Model the rabbits eating grasses. Have each rabbit try to obtain 20 beans from the grass plants. Do all the rabbits survive? Is there extra energy?

**STEP 4** Leave 2 beans on each rabbit to represent the energy stored in each rabbit's body. Set the rest of the beans aside to represent energy used by the rabbits and transferred to the environment as heat.

**STEP 5** Model the fox eating rabbits. Have the fox try to obtain 30 beans from the rabbits. Were there enough rabbits to support the fox? How many more rabbits will the food chain need to support two foxes?

**STEP 6** **Do the Math** What percentage of all the sun's energy provided to the grass plants was available to the rabbit population? What percentage of all energy provided by grass plants to the rabbits was available to the fox?

**STEP 7** Return to Step 1 to run the model again using the weasel instead of the fox. Does the weasel survive? Given the energy available from the sun, which animal can be successful in this ecosystem—the fox or the weasel?

**STEP 8** Why are some organisms more numerous in the ecosystem than others? Use numbers from the modeling activity to support your answer.

### MATERIALS

- index cards (18), labeled: sun (1), grass plants (10), rabbits (5), fox (1), weasel (1)
- resealable bags (10), each holding 100 dried beans

### MODEL PARAMETERS

- Energy is represented in the model by the packets of beans. One packet of 100 beans is required to support one grass plant.
- 20 beans are required to support one rabbit.
- 30 beans are required to support one fox.
- 10 beans are required to support one weasel.

## Energy Pyramids

When an organism obtains energy, most of the energy is used for life processes. Some of the energy is given off to the environment as heat. A small amount of energy is stored in an organism's body. Only this stored energy can be used by a consumer that eats the organism.

An **energy pyramid** is a representation of the energy available at each level of a food web. The shape of the energy pyramid shows that there is less energy available at each level. The number of organisms that can be supported at each level is limited by the amount of energy available. The bottom level—the producers—has the most energy. The other levels are consumers. Consumers at the highest level have the least amount of available energy.

The shape of this energy pyramid shows that the energy available decreases as you move up this arctic tundra food chain.

8. Explain how energy is conserved even though the amount of energy available decreases as you move up the pyramid.

 **EVIDENCE NOTEBOOK**

9. What happens to producer populations in Yellowstone when elk and deer populations become smaller? How might these changes explain the increase in the beaver population? Record your evidence.

## Describe Energy Transfer between Ecosystems

10. Ecosystems do not have clear boundaries—matter and energy can move from one ecosystem to another. The energy available in ecosystems is constant / constantly changing. As grass-seeking wildebeest migrate from the Serengeti of Tanzania to Kenya each year, the energy available in the Serengeti ecosystem increases / decreases.

11. **Collaborate** With a partner, brainstorm about other ways in which matter and energy might move from one ecosystem to another.

These wildebeest move matter and energy from one ecosystem to another as they cross the Mara River in Tanzania.

_____

_____

_____

# Describing the Cycling of Matter in Ecosystems

## Energy Drives the Cycling of Matter

Driven by the flow of energy, matter cycles through both the living and nonliving parts of ecosystems. As one organism eats another organism in a food web, both energy and matter are transferred to the body of the consumer. Eventually, the matter that makes up the bodies of living things is returned to the environment by decomposers.

12. **Discuss** In any system, energy is required to move matter. For example, windmills require wind energy. Spinning car wheels require engines. Water turbines require moving water. With a partner, think of some other ways that energy can be used to drive circular motion.

## The Water Cycle

Water moves continuously through Earth's systems, including ecosystems. The force of gravity drags massive glaciers, pulls raindrops from clouds, and draws streams into lakes and oceans. The sun's energy melts ice and causes water to evaporate into the air. Wind then carries it across sea and land. Water also moves through living things, where its flows into and out of cells. Organisms use energy when they take water from the Earth system and when they release it. Wherever water moves, energy is at work.

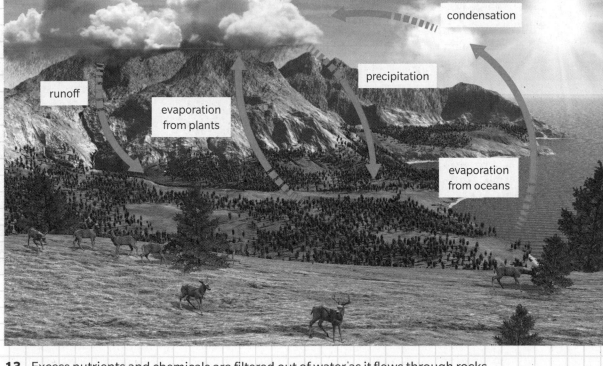

13. Excess nutrients and chemicals are filtered out of water as it flows through rocks and soil. When natural surfaces are replaced by pavement, the amount of chemical pollutants that reach lakes and oceans is likely to decrease / increase.

14. Decreased plant growth near a river can result in excess soil entering and clogging the water. How might the wolves help increase the plant growth that stabilizes the rivers the beavers rely on to live?

## The Carbon Cycle

Carbon is essential to life because all cells are made of carbon-based molecules. Organisms obtain more than energy from food. They also gain carbon and other elements needed for growth and life. The carbon cycle makes this possible when physical and chemical changes transfer carbon between the environment and living cells.

Photosynthesis, cellular respiration, and the digestion of food are processes that cycle carbon between the environment, food molecules, and cells. Decomposition is also part of the carbon cycle. Decomposition returns carbon stored in the remains of organisms to the environment. These transfers of carbon are driven by the energy flowing through ecosystem food webs.

Energy also drives carbon transfers between land, water, and air, without using living organisms. Human activities affect some of these transfers. Burning fossil fuels speeds up the transfer of carbon from the earth to the air. Cutting down forests slows down the transfer of carbon from the air to living things. These changes affect the stability of ecosystems over time.

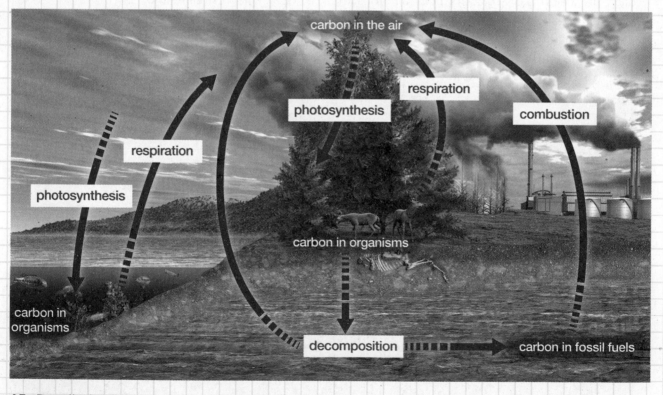

© Houghton Mifflin Harcourt

15. Describe how carbon enters and exits a consumer, such as the deer shown in the diagram.

## Engineer It
# Analyze a Solution

Artificial trees are human-made systems engineered to collect carbon pollutants from the air. These systems can be used in locations where it may be difficult to grow real trees, such as dense, urban areas. Artificial trees can be powered by wind and solar energy. They can also be powered with energy generated by swings or seesaws that are attached to the system. The energy generated by the motion of people swinging can be transferred to the artificial tree and used to power the carbon collection process.

This tower removes carbon from the air and compresses it into cubes that are used to make jewelery. The profits from the sale of the jewelery are used to make more towers.

16. Trees use the carbon dioxide they get from the environment to make water / sugar / oxygen that stores energy. Like trees, engineers could find a way to use captured carbon dioxide to make fuel / sugar / water that stores energy.

## The Nitrogen Cycle

Cells use nitrogen to build many life molecules, including DNA. Bacteria in soil and water change nitrogen into chemical forms that plants and algae can use. Nitrogen enters most food webs when plants or algae take up these forms of nitrogen. Decomposers return nitrogen to the soil and water, where bacteria can change it back to a gas form, returning it to air.

nitrogen from air

bacteria change nitrogen back to gas

nitrogen from rabbit

nitrogen in plants

bacteria change nitrogen into usable form

nitrogen absorbed by plant roots

nitrogen in dead organisms

17. All organisms need a source of nitrogen and other matter. Explain how the nitrogen and other matter in your body came from other living things and the environment.

# Diagram the Cycling of Matter

Eagles prefer to eat fish. Therefore, they tend to live in forested borders of inland lakes and rocky shorelines of North America. They also feed on turtles and other reptiles, rodents, and dead animals. As lakes freeze over in winter, the eagles migrate to warmer areas. Their diet switches to include more birds, which are easier to find during cold months.

Explore ONLINE!

**18. Draw** Make a diagram of the flow of carbon in the eagle's winter or summer food chain. Include producers and other consumers. Use arrows to indicate the cycling of carbon through the living and nonliving parts of the ecosystem.

**19.** Describe how the eagle is involved in the movement of matter within and between ecosystems.

_____
_____
_____
_____
_____
_____
_____

# Continue Your Exploration

Name: _____          Date: _____

**Check out the path below or go online to choose one of the other paths shown.**

**People in Science**

- **Hands-On Labs** 👋
- **Biomagnification**
- **Propose Your Own Path**

Go online to choose one of these other paths.

## Charles Elton, Ecologist

Charles Elton was an English biologist who lived during the early 1900s. He is credited with establishing ecology as a scientific field. He gathered a large amount of data to draw conclusions about ecosystem populations. Before Elton's work, most people studied the natural world by observing and describing, rather than experimenting and collecting data. Elton discovered that food chains display a "pyramid of numbers." That is, producers have the largest population sizes and top consumers have the smallest population sizes. Later scientists built upon Elton's work to develop the energy pyramid model used today to represent the amount of energy available at each feeding level.

One of Elton's later books described the ecology of voles. Voles are a favorite meal for birds of prey. Their populations rise and fall wildly in different ecosystems. This made the voles an intriguing subject for Elton. He spent his life to trying to explain ecosystem dynamics using reliable numbers.

1. Charles Elton needed to gather data from several different ecosystems to be certain that the pyramid of numbers explains a real pattern in food chains. What does this tell you about the connection between the nature of science and the use of evidence?

A hungry owl catches a vole. An owl might eat up to three voles each day.

# Continue Your Exploration

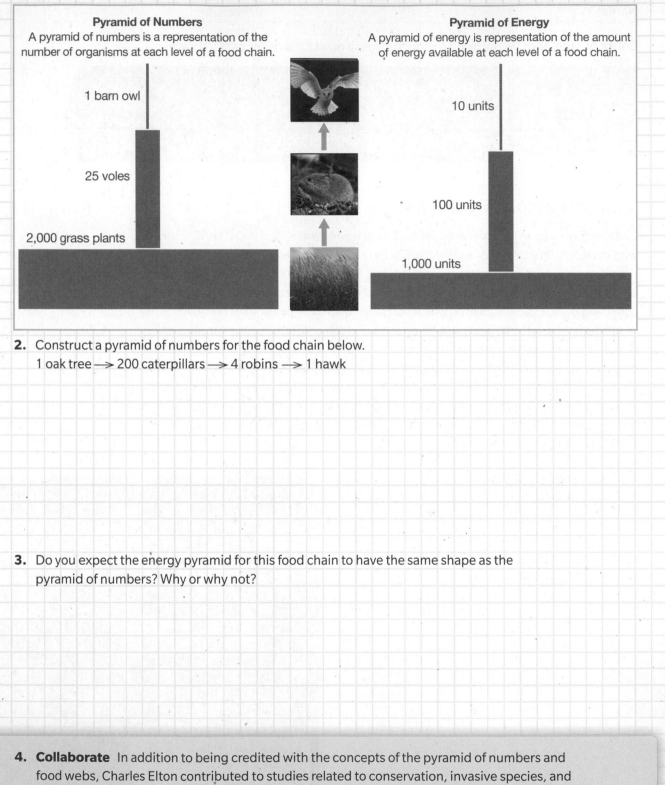

### Pyramid of Numbers
A pyramid of numbers is a representation of the number of organisms at each level of a food chain.

1 barn owl

25 voles

2,000 grass plants

### Pyramid of Energy
A pyramid of energy is representation of the amount of energy available at each level of a food chain.

10 units

100 units

1,000 units

2. Construct a pyramid of numbers for the food chain below.

    1 oak tree ⟶ 200 caterpillars ⟶ 4 robins ⟶ 1 hawk

3. Do you expect the energy pyramid for this food chain to have the same shape as the pyramid of numbers? Why or why not?

4. **Collaborate** In addition to being credited with the concepts of the pyramid of numbers and food webs, Charles Elton contributed to studies related to conservation, invasive species, and wildlife disease ecology. Work with a classmate to research the career of Charles Elton. Present your biography as a multimedia presentation. Lead a post-presentation discussion about how Charles Elton's methods may have influenced new generations of ecologists.

# Can You Explain It?

**55**

**Name:** _____     **Date:** _____

**How could the reintroduction of wolves to Yellowstone have led to an increase in the beaver population?**

Explore
ONLINE!

**EVIDENCE NOTEBOOK**

Refer to the notes in your Evidence Notebook to help you construct an explanation for how the reintroduction of wolves to Yellowstone influenced the park's beaver population.

1. State your claim. Make sure your claim fully explains why the beaver population increased after wolves were reintroduced to Yellowstone National Park.

2. Summarize the evidence you have gathered to support your claim and explain your reasoning.

# Checkpoints

Answer the following questions to check your understanding of the lesson.

Use the photo to answer Questions 3–4.

3. Ants eat a variety of foods, including plants and other insects. A reptile called a *thorny devil* eats ants. If a food chain that includes the thorny devil and ants is represented by an energy pyramid, the ants would occupy the
bottom / middle / top pyramid level.

thorny devil

4. Which statement about thorny devils and ants is true?

   A. The thorny devil stores almost all of the energy it receives from eating ants.

   B. Thorny devils get all the matter they need from eating ants.

   C. There is likely an equal number of ants and thorny devils in the desert ecosystem.

   D. Carbon and other nonliving materials flow from ants to thorny devils as ants are eaten.

---

Use the photo to answer Question 5.

5. Which statement(s) describe how the river moves matter between land and water ecosystems? Select all that apply.

   A. The river provides water to many land animals.

   B. The river draws soil nutrients into water for use by aquatic plants.

   C. The pull of gravity allows water to move from where it falls as rain, returning it to the ocean.

   D. Rivers carry rocks downstream.

---

6. What processes drive the flow of carbon between living and nonliving components of ecosystems? Select all that apply.

   A. photosynthesis

   B. evaporation

   C. decomposition

   D. cellular respiration

# Interactive Review

**Complete this section to review the main concepts of the lesson.**

Energy is transferred in ecosystems through a network of producers, consumers, and decomposers that are connected.

**A.** Use a concept map to illustrate the role of producers, consumers, and decomposers in the transfer of energy through ecosystems

Matter continuously cycles between the living and nonliving parts of an ecosystem. The flow of energy drives the cycling of matter through ecosystems.

**B.** The water, carbon, and nitrogen cycles share patterns in the flow of matter and energy through ecosystems. Describe two different patterns that can be observed in all three cycles.

**Choose one of the activities to explore how this unit connects to other topics.**

## ☐ Physical Science Connection

**Energy Transformations**  An energy transformation takes place when energy changes from one form to another. For example, plants transform light energy from the sun into chemical energy stored in the bonds of sugar molecules. The Hoover Dam transforms the mechanical energy of rushing water into electrical energy that can be used by homes, offices, and buildings within the region.

Using library or Internet sources, research three different examples of energy transformation. Identify the primary forms of energy involved in each transformation. Use visuals to present your findings.

Hoover Dam

## ☐ Health Connection

**The Gluten-Free Craze**  Looking around a grocery store, many products are labeled "gluten-free." A gluten-free diet is recommended to help people with certain immune disorders. The gluten-free trend has also been adopted by other people as a way to lose weight and increase energy levels. However, these claims have not been proven by research.

Using library or Internet sources, find out what gluten is. Research the effects of adopting a gluten-free diet. Create a poster or other visual display that explains how a gluten-free diet could affect a person's energy levels.

## ☐ Art Connection

**Seeing Red with Green Plants**  Some photographers use different types of film and filters to produce interesting effects. For example, the photograph shown here is an example of infrared photography. This technique lets certain parts of the light spectrum pass through the camera, while blocking other parts of the spectrum. For green plants, the result is a deep red color.

Using library and Internet resources, research why we see light as different colors, and explain why plants usually look green. Then compare visible light to infrared light. Explain why using infrared film and filters can make the same plants appear red. Create a multimedia presentation that explains your findings.

Name: _____ Date: _____

**Complete this review to check your understanding of the unit.**

**Use the graph to answer Questions 1–3.**

1. What conclusions can be made about the rate of photosynthesis shown in the graph? Select all that apply.

   A. The rate of photosynthesis changes over a day

   B. The rate of photosynthesis decreases at night.

   C. The rate of photosynthesis decreases at midday.

   D. The rate of photosynthesis is lowest only at 10 p.m.

   E. The rate of photosynthesis is constant.

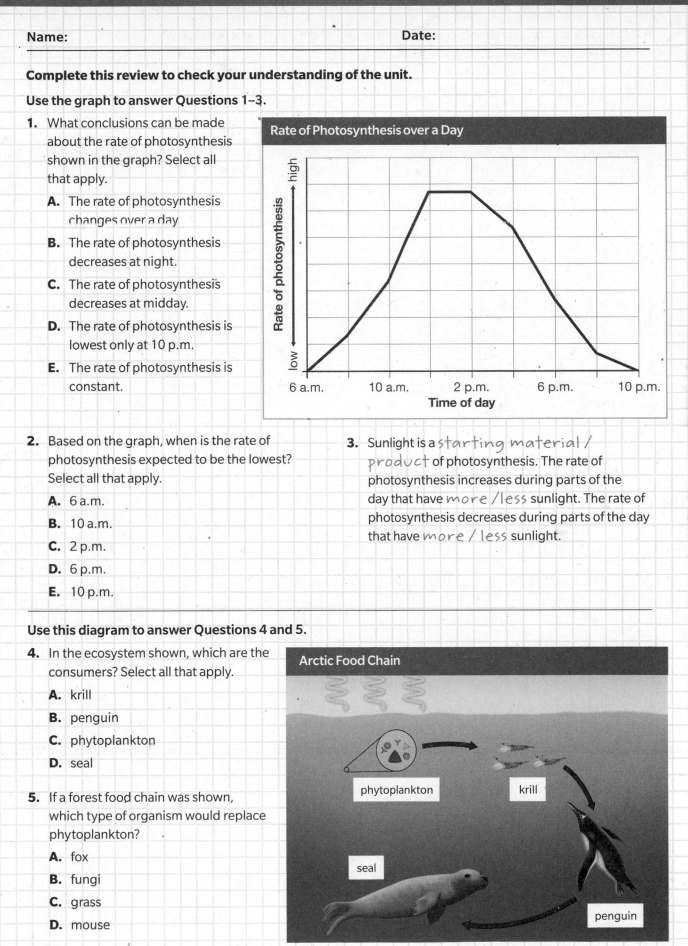

Rate of Photosynthesis over a Day

2. Based on the graph, when is the rate of photosynthesis expected to be the lowest? Select all that apply.

   A. 6 a.m.

   B. 10 a.m.

   C. 2 p.m.

   D. 6 p.m.

   E. 10 p.m.

3. Sunlight is a starting material / product of photosynthesis. The rate of photosynthesis increases during parts of the day that have more /less sunlight. The rate of photosynthesis decreases during parts of the day that have more / less sunlight.

---

**Use this diagram to answer Questions 4 and 5.**

4. In the ecosystem shown, which are the consumers? Select all that apply.

   A. krill

   B. penguin

   C. phytoplankton

   D. seal

5. If a forest food chain was shown, which type of organism would replace phytoplankton?

   A. fox

   B. fungi

   C. grass

   D. mouse

Arctic Food Chain

phytoplankton

krill

seal

penguin

**6.** Complete the table by describing the flow of energy and the cycling of matter at different scales of living systems.

| Scale | Flow of Energy | Cycling of Matter |
|---|---|---|
| Plant and Animal Cells | Plant cells use light energy from the sun to produce sugar molecules through photosynthesis. Plant and animal cells release the energy stored in sugar molecules during cellular respiration. This energy is used for life processes. | |
| Organisms | | |
| Ecosystems | | |

Name: _____     Date: _____

**Use the diagram to answer Questions 7–9.**

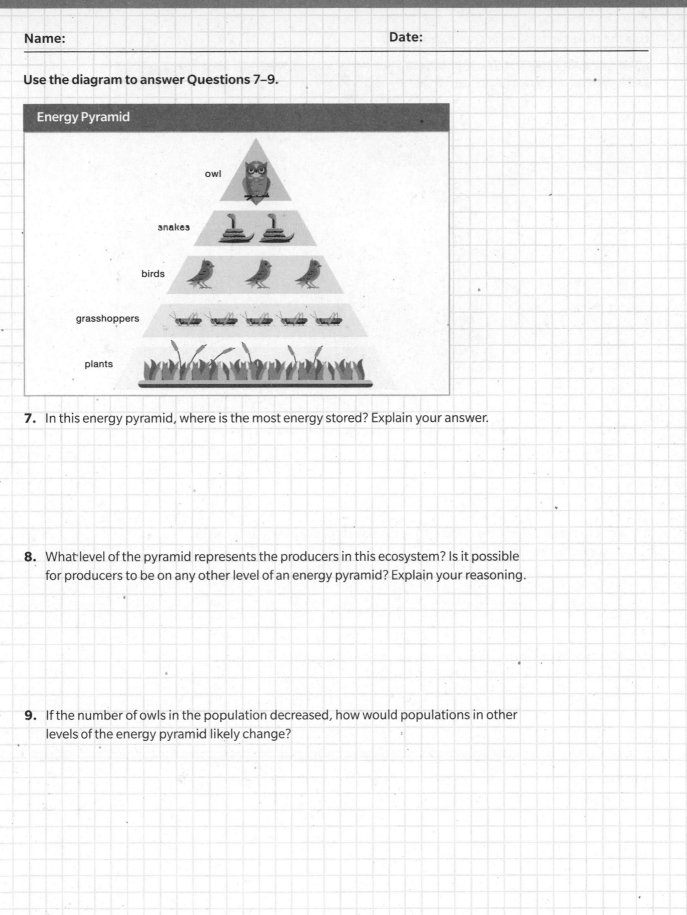

Energy Pyramid

owl

snakes

birds

grasshoppers

plants

**7.** In this energy pyramid, where is the most energy stored? Explain your answer.

**8.** What level of the pyramid represents the producers in this ecosystem? Is it possible for producers to be on any other level of an energy pyramid? Explain your reasoning.

**9.** If the number of owls in the population decreased, how would populations in other levels of the energy pyramid likely change?

**Use the diagram to answer Questions 10–13.**

### Photosynthesis Investigation

In this investigation, a plant is contained in water with a light shining down on it. Wire tubing connects the container to a syringe that measures oxygen production, which can be seen in the container in the form of oxygen bubbles.

**10.** Explain how this investigation can be used to observe photosynthesis.

**11.** Which reactants (starting materials) and products of photosynthesis can be observed in this diagram?

**12.** How would you expect the amount of oxygen to change if the intensity of the light is increased or decreased? Explain your reasoning.

**13.** Explain why plants such as this one need to perform both photosynthesis and cellular respiration to survive.

Name: _____  Date: _____

# Should your school use vermicomposting?

Composting has been used for many years. In this process, food and yard waste is saved to decompose and create a rich, fertile soil. Vermicomposting is one method of composting that has become popular recently. Your task is to help determine if vermicomposting would be a good option for food waste from your school's cafeteria.

Research the use of vermicomposting units. Explain how a vermicomposting unit works, describe the flow of energy and cycling of matter within the system, and determine the advantages and disadvantages of using this type of system to dispose of food waste from your school's cafeteria.

### Vermicomposter

This vermicomposter shows a three-bin system for using worms to decompose food and yard waste into a nutrient-rich mixture that can be added to soil.

cover
holes for air
bedding material
food waste and worms (active area)
storage bin
compost
compost collection
brick support

**The steps below will help guide your research and develop your recommendation.**

### Engineer It

1. **Define the Problem**  Write a statement defining the problem you have been asked to solve. Define the criteria and constraints of the design problems based on what is reasonable for your school and the cafeteria.

## Engineer It

2. **Conduct Research**  What is vermicomposting? Explain how worms break down food waste and how the compost that is produced can be used.

3. **Develop a Model**  Use a labeled diagram or another model of a vermicomposting unit to describe the function of each layer and explain how energy and matter flow through the system.

4. **Make a Recommendation**  List the advantages and disadvantages of using a vermicomposting unit. Write a recommendation that explains whether this would be a good solution for disposing of food waste from your school.

5. **Communicate**  Create a multimedia presentation of your findings to present to the principal. Use your labeled diagram or model to summarize how vermicomposting works, and explain whether or not you should use vermicomposting at your school. Provide evidence and reasoning for your recommendation.

## ✓ Self-Check

| | |
|---|---|
| | I defined the criteria and constraints of the design problem. |
| | I researched the process of vermicomposting to determine the advantages and disadvantages. |
| | I used a diagram or model to explain the function of each layer in a vermicomposting unit and how energy and matter flow through the unit. |
| | My recommendation was clearly communicated during my presentation. |

# Relationships in Ecosystems

This coyote roams the Sonoran Desert near Tucson, Arizona. The coyote's diet varies with the seasons in the desert, based on the availability of different food resources.

Whether in the desert, arctic, or rain forest, all ecosystems have living and nonliving parts. Organisms rely on different parts of their environment to provide resources for survival. For example, coyotes in the Sonoran Desert often make their den under rock outcroppings or bushes. Depending on the season, these coyotes may eat cactus fruit, insects, rodents, or lizards. Scientists study ecosystem interactions to make predictions about populations and to assess an ecosystem's health. In this unit, you will investigate how resource availability affects populations and how organisms interact.

# Why It Matters

Here are some questions to consider as you work through the unit. Can you answer any of the questions now? Revisit these questions at the end of the unit to apply what you discover.

| Questions | Notes |
|---|---|
| What are the living and nonliving things that can be found in your neighborhood? | |
| What are the basic things you need to survive? What does a houseplant need to survive? | |
| Why do living things need these resources? | |
| What would happen if one of these resources was no longer available? | |
| What are some types of organisms on which humans rely? | |
| What would happen if the population of one of these organisms increased or decreased? | |

## Unit Starter: Analyzing Duck Population Size

This graph shows the duck population size from 1955 through 2015 in North America.

*Source*: U.S. Fish and Wildlife Service 2014 Report

1. According to the graph, the duck population increased / decreased between 1965 and 1970 and increased / decreased between 2000 and 2005.

2. What factors might cause duck populations to increase? Select all that apply.
   A. improvements made to duck habitats, such as restored wetlands
   B. below normal snowfall in winter that leads to increased access to food
   C. early warm spring temperatures that allow for early nesting and reproduction
   D. flooding in wetlands during the spring and summer limits nesting sites

*Go online to download the Unit Project Worksheet to help you plan your project.*

## Unit Project

# How Organisms Interact

How do organisms interact with each other in an ecosystem? Research an ecosystem, and identify specific interactions that occur within it. Learn about the organisms involved in each interaction, and evaluate their importance in the functioning of the ecosystem. Identify a resource in the ecosystem, and analyze how changes in its availability would impact these interactions. Present your findings in a multimedia presentation.

© Houghton Mifflin Harcourt

# Parts of an Ecosystem

The living and nonliving parts of a coral reef provide food and shelter to millions of organisms.

**By the end of this lesson . . .**

you will be able to relate the needs of organisms to the levels of organization in an ecosystem.

© Houghton Mifflin Harcourt • Image Credits: ©Darryl Leniuk/DigitalVision/Getty Images

**Go online** to view the digital version of the Hands-On Lab for this lesson and to download additional lab resources.

# CAN YOU EXPLAIN IT?

### How is your schoolyard similar to this tundra ecosystem?

The tundra has a layer of subsoil that is permanently frozen. Summers are very short, and winters are cold, windy, and long.

**1.** What living and nonliving things have you observed in your schoolyard?

**2.** How do you think the living and nonliving parts of your schoolyard interact?

**EVIDENCE NOTEBOOK** As you explore the lesson, gather evidence to help explain how your schoolyard is similar to a tundra ecosystem.

# Analyzing Parts of an Ecosystem

An **ecosystem** is all the organisms living together in a particular place along with their nonliving environment. Ecosystems contain everything that organisms need to survive. Think about an earthworm living in a yard. The earthworm interacts with other living things when it eats fallen leaves for food or when a predator captures it. The earthworm also needs air and water, which are nonliving parts of the ecosystem.

A parent robin feeds its chicks a meal of worms.

3. **Discuss** Together with a partner, discuss how these baby birds are interacting with the living and nonliving parts of their environment.

## Forest Ecosystem

As you explore this forest ecosystem, look at the photos and descriptions on the next page to learn more about how these organisms interact with their environment.

A flying squirrel glides from tree to tree using the flaps of skin that extend from its front legs to its hind legs. It eats a variety of foods, including the seeds and nuts produced by plants.

Many different organisms, such as this salmon, depend on this stream for oxygen, nutrients, shelter, and water.

Shelf fungi absorb nutrients and minerals from decaying plants and animals. The part of the fungus you can see on the tree bark is just a small part of the whole organism. Microscopic fungal projections extend deep into the log.

The soil of the forest floor contains nutrients and water that living things, such as earthworms and plants, need. It also provides shelter for burrowing animals, such as moles.

**4.** Look at the picture of a forest ecosystem. In the table below, record at least five living and five nonliving parts of this ecosystem.

| Living | Nonliving |
|---|---|
|  |  |
|  |  |

 **EVIDENCE NOTEBOOK**

**5.** Explain whether or not your schoolyard is an ecosystem. Record your evidence.

# The Living Environment

The parts of an ecosystem that are living, or that result from the activities of living things, are called **biotic factors**. For example, think about a dragonfly that lives in a meadow near a pond. Biotic factors in the dragonfly's ecosystem include the tadpoles, green algae, and insects that the dragonfly eats. Green plants are also biotic factors—dragonflies lay their eggs on the leaves of plants. Other biotic factors that interact with the dragonfly are the animals that eat dragonflies, such as fish, salamanders, and frogs, and other insects that compete with dragonflies for food. A decaying log that dragonflies perch on would also be considered a biotic factor since it is the remains of a living thing.

# The Nonliving Environment

An **abiotic factor** is a nonliving part of an ecosystem. Some abiotic factors are air, nutrients, soil, sunlight, water, wind, and temperature. A dragonfly spends the first part of its life cycle in the water. The water must be a certain temperature for the young dragonfly to survive. The adult dragonfly also needs a certain air temperature to be able to fly. Both young and adult dragonflies need oxygen to breathe.

**Language SmArts**
## Identify Relationships

Prairie dogs live in underground burrows and eat mostly plants. The prairie dogs work together to make burrows. Individuals take turns looking out for animals that could eat them. Predators of prairie dogs include coyotes, badgers, bobcats, and birds of prey such as falcons and eagles.

6. **Draw** Create a flow chart that shows the interactions among the living and nonliving factors related to prairie dogs.

# Describing Ecosystem Structure

The bodies of individuals, including you and your friends, can be described according to different levels of organization, from the smallest living unit—a cell—to a whole organism made up of interacting body systems. This soccer player, for example, drinks water that will move through the digestive system and eventually reach millions of cells in the athlete's body.

Ecosystems can also be described according to their levels of organization. Ecosystems can be organized from the simplest component, an individual organism, to the entire ecosystem.

This athlete drinks water that will end up in the body's cells.

7. An individual organism is the smallest level of organization in an ecosystem. Think about the levels of organization in an organism. Order the levels in the word bank from smallest to largest.

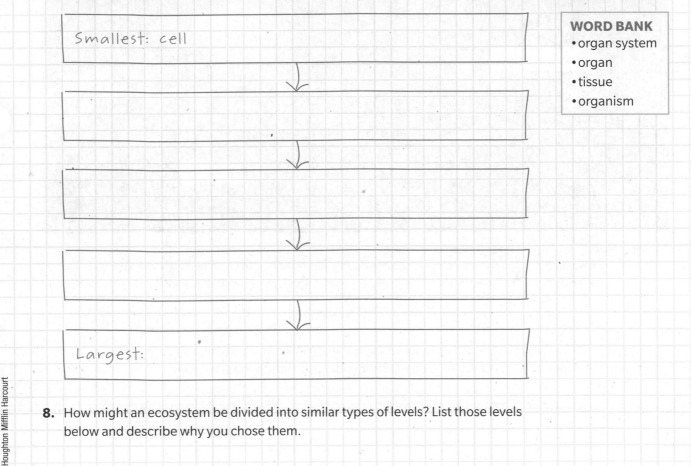

Smallest: cell

Largest:

**WORD BANK**
- organ system
- organ
- tissue
- organism

8. How might an ecosystem be divided into similar types of levels? List those levels below and describe why you chose them.

# Levels of Organization in Ecosystems

An ecosystem can be organized into different levels. The smallest level is a single organism. The largest level is the entire ecosystem—all of the organisms in an area along with their surroundings. Each level of organization gets more complex as more of the environment is considered.

**Florida Everglades Ecosystem**

This Florida Everglades ecosystem includes communities of living organisms and nonliving factors such as water, soil, rocks, and air.

osprey

great blue herons

alligators

**Individual**
An individual is a single organism, such as one alligator, one heron, or one tree.

**Population**
All the great blue herons in the ecosystem make up a population of herons. All the trees in the Everglades do not make up a population because there are trees of many different species there.

**Community**
This community includes populations of alligators, great blue herons, osprey, fish, trees, grasses, and microscopic organisms such as bacteria and algae.

9. Choose an organism from the picture above. Name the organism and then describe at least three interactions it has with either biotic or abiotic factors in the ecosystem.

## Individual

An individual is a single organism, such as one alligator. Each type of organism belongs to a different species. A **species** includes organisms that are of the same kind and can successfully reproduce, resulting in fertile offspring.

## Population

A **population** is a group of individuals of the same species that live in the same place at the same time. Individuals within a population often compete with each other for resources. An example is the alligators in the Everglades ecosystem that compete for food, space, and mates.

## Community

A **community** is made up of all the populations of different species that live and interact in an area. The species in a community depend on each other for many things, such as shelter and food. For example, animals get energy and nutrients by eating other organisms.

Populations in a community compete with other populations for resources. One example is two bird populations with similar nesting habits that may compete for nesting space. Two populations with similar diets may compete for food resources.

## Ecosystem

An ecosystem is a community of organisms and their nonliving environment, such as the Everglades ecosystem. Energy flows through an ecosystem, starting with sunlight that powers plant and algal growth. Energy continues to flow through the ecosystem as one organism eats another. Ecosystems occur at all scales, from a tiny puddle to a vast forest.

© Houghton Mifflin Harcourt

**EVIDENCE NOTEBOOK**

**10.** How do the levels of organization in the tundra ecosystem relate to the levels of organization in your schoolyard? Record your evidence.

## African Savanna Ecosystem

**11.** Build levels of organization in this savanna ecosystem, starting with an individual giraffe. Write each biotic or abiotic factor in the circle in which it belongs. If a factor has been written in an inner circle, it is automatically included in each larger circle.

**WORD BANK**
- all giraffes
- water
- air
- elephants
- grasses
- soil
- rocks
- trees
- shrubs
- minerals and nutrients in the water and soil

**ecosystem**

**community**

**population**

**individual**

single giraffe

## Hands-On Lab
# Investigate Your Schoolyard

You will plan an investigation to answer a question about environmental factors in your schoolyard.

## Procedure and Analysis

**STEP 1** Use a meterstick to measure a 3 m x 3 m area to study. Push craft sticks in the ground to mark the corners of the site. Tie the string to the sticks to create a boundary around your site.

**STEP 2** Observe your study area. Ask a question that involves one or more parts of the environment that you observe. Remember that the environment includes both living and nonliving factors.

**STEP 3** On a separate sheet of paper, plan an investigation to answer your question. Your procedure might include

- recording qualitative data such as descriptions and sketches

- recording quantitative data such as counts of organisms

- staking out a smaller area to observe in greater detail

- collecting a sample of soil or leaf debris to observe with a hand lens

**STEP 4** Have your teacher approve your plan. Carry out your procedure.

**STEP 5** Summarize your data.

**STEP 6** Are you able to answer your question? If so, construct an explanation that answers your question, using evidence from your investigation. If not, explain how you could modify your procedure to better answer your question.

| MATERIALS |
| --- |
| • craft sticks (at least 4) |
| • field guides to local plants and animals |
| • forceps |
| • hand lenses, 3X and 6X |
| • markers or colored pencils, several different colors |
| • meterstick or tape measure |
| • notebook |
| • paper cups |
| • paper, white unlined |
| • pen or pencil |
| • string (15 m) |
| • thermometer, pH paper, optional |
| • trowels, forks, and/or spoons |

**EVIDENCE NOTEBOOK**

**12.** What factors did you observe in your schoolyard that might be similar to factors in the tundra ecosystem? Record your evidence.

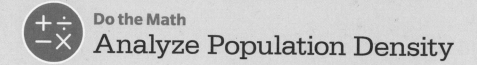

## Do the Math
# Analyze Population Density

The forests around La Selva, Costa Rica, have been changing. The amount of dead leaves, or leaf litter, on the forest floor is decreasing. This may be due to increases in rainfall, which can result in fewer leaves falling. Native pigs may also be destroying leaves more quickly. Either way, this could cause problems for poison dart frogs that live in the leaf litter.

Below are data from an experiment to test the hypothesis that changes in leaf litter will affect the populations of poison dart frogs. The data are counts of frogs present when leaf litter was unchanged, leaves were added, or leaves were removed. The experiment was repeated ten times. Use the data to determine if changes in leaf litter affect poison dart frogs on the forest floor.

| Counts of Strawberry Poison Dart Frogs | | | |
|---|---|---|---|
| Trial | No change | Leaves added | Leaves removed |
| 1 | 5 | 10 | 2 |
| 2 | 4 | 15 | 0 |
| 3 | 7 | 3 | 1 |
| 4 | 4 | 18 | 1 |
| 5 | 5 | 15 | 2 |
| 6 | 6 | 8 | 9 |
| 7 | 16 | 12 | 0 |
| 8 | 6 | 14 | 3 |
| 9 | 8 | 17 | 0 |
| 10 | 6 | 11 | 2 |
| Average | | | |

Strawberry poison dart frogs live in leaf litter on the forest floor.

13. Calculate the average frog count for each treatment. Write the averages in the table.

14. What patterns do you see in the data? Are changes in the amount of leaf litter a threat to strawberry poison dart frogs? Support your answer with evidence from the data.

_____

_____

_____

15. **Engineer It** Propose a solution for how the ecosystem might be restored. What factors need to be considered when restoring an ecosystem?

_____

_____

_____

_____

_____

# Continue Your Exploration

Name: _____ Date: _____

**Check out the path below or go online to choose one of the other paths shown.**

People in Science

- **Hands-On Labs** 🖐
- **Biome Guided Research**
- **Propose Your Own Path**

*Go online to choose one of these other paths.*

## Dr. Kenneth Krysko, Wildlife Ecologist

Can you imagine a career studying the interactions of organisms in the environment? You might have a job like Dr. Kenneth Krysko, an ecologist who tracks Burmese pythons to help limit the effects they have on Florida ecosystems. These pythons were illegally brought to Florida as pets decades ago. Some of the pythons escaped or were released into the environment when people didn't want them anymore. Their population has expanded greatly as the snakes eat just about any animal small enough to swallow.

Dr. Krysko shares what he learns with other ecologists. Through wildlife management, genetics, and other areas of study, Dr. Krysko works with other scientists to find ways to reduce the size of the python population.

# Continue Your Exploration

1. Dr. Krysko works in the Florida Everglades. Where else might ecologists work? Give at least three examples.

2. Describe how Dr. Krysko's work relates to each level of organization in the Everglades ecosystem.

3. Describe three types of ecosystems where you might like to work. Explain why you chose each ecosystem.

4. **Collaborate** Work with other students to learn about a career as an ecologist. With your teacher's guidance, contact an ecologist working in your area for an interview. Prepare your questions ahead of time. Ask the ecologist about the education and coursework needed for this career, the questions and topics that are studied, and the impact of his or her work. Write your interview in a question/answer format.

# Can You Explain It?

Name: _____     Date: _____

How is your schoolyard similar to this tundra ecosystem?

**EVIDENCE NOTEBOOK**

Refer to the notes in your Evidence Notebook to help you construct an explanation for how your schoolyard is similar to a tundra.

1. State your claim. Make sure your claim fully explains the similarities between the tundra and your schoolyard.

2. Summarize the evidence you have gathered to support your claim and explain your reasoning.

# Checkpoints

**Answer the following questions to check your understanding of the lesson.**

**Use the photo to answer Questions 3 and 4.**

3. Which statement most completely summarizes how the sea dragon pictured here interacts with its environment?

   **A.** It interacts only with other animals.

   **B.** It interacts with a variety of living and nonliving factors.

   **C.** It gets oxygen from the water and takes shelter in seaweeds.

4. Select any items from this list that are abiotic factors in the sea dragon's ecosystem.

   **A.** water

   **B.** nutrients dissolved in the water

   **C.** seaweeds

   **D.** sand and rocks on the sea floor

---

**Use the picture to answer Questions 5 and 6.**

5. Which factors are included in a forest community? Select all that apply.

   **A.** every squirrel in the forest

   **B.** all of the forest's populations

   **C.** plants, fungi, and microbes in the forest

   **D.** rushing stream

   **E.** rock on which turtles and frogs sit

6. Which option describes how the fish in the picture interacts with abiotic factors in the ecosystem? Select all that apply.

   **A.** The fish swims in the water.

   **B.** The owl eats the fish.

   **C.** The fish breathes oxygen in the water.

   **D.** The fish lays eggs on water plants.

   **E.** The fish eats water bugs.

# Interactive Review

**Complete this section to review the main concepts of the lesson.**

An ecosystem contains both living and nonliving components.

**A.** Describe the living and nonliving parts of an ecosystem of your choice.

An ecosystem's structure can be described according to levels of organization.

**B.** Describe the levels of organization in an ecosystem of your choice.

# Resource Availability in Ecosystems

This coniferous forest provides resources such as food and shelter for a wide variety of organisms.

**By the end of this lesson . . .**

you will be able to predict the impact of resource availability on the growth of organisms and populations in an ecosystem.

# CAN YOU EXPLAIN IT?

## How does a wildfire affect resources and populations in a forest?

Some wildfires are caused by humans, but fires can also start because of a natural factor such as a lightning strike.

 *Explore ONLINE!*

1. Imagine that you saw a huge green forest one day, and the next day you saw the scene in the photo above. Describe what you observe in this photo.

2. Think about all the organisms that live in a forest. How do you think living things were affected by this fire?

 **EVIDENCE NOTEBOOK** As you explore this lesson, gather evidence to help explain how a wildfire affects resources and populations in a forest ecosystem.

# Relating Resource Availability to Growth

You may think you are very different from a hummingbird or an earthworm, but humans, hummingbirds, and earthworms all have the same basic needs. In fact, *all* organisms require the same basic resources to survive, grow, develop, respond to the environment, and reproduce. Can you think of what some of these key resources are?

3.  Water is a resource that all organisms need, including plants. If a plant does not receive water for an extended period, the plant  will / will not  be able to perform life functions. As a result, the plant will  continue / stop  growing and will eventually  reproduce / die  without water.

4.  In the table below, record your observations for each image. Then write the label that best matches what is happening in each image: lack of water, sufficient water, too much water.

## Growth Requires Resources

All living things must get resources from their environment so that their cells have a source of materials and energy. The resources that organisms need to live and grow include food, water, and shelter. Some of these resources are living. Food and some types of shelter, such as a tree, are living resources. Water and some types of shelter, such as a burrow in the ground or rock crevices, are nonliving resources. Sunlight and soil are also nonliving resources. Organisms get all of the living and nonliving resources they need from the ecosystem in which they live. The growth of both individuals and populations depends on resource availability within an ecosystem.

## Individual Growth

A hatchling from a tiny egg can become a large sea turtle, and an acorn can grow into a towering tree. These individual organisms—like all individual organisms—require resources to grow. Only with sufficient resources can an individual survive, grow, and eventually reproduce.

## Population Growth

The growth of a population also depends on the availability of resources, including food, water, and shelter. Suppose that the organisms in an ecosystem have an abundance of the resources that they need to grow and reproduce. Under these conditions, the number of organisms in a population will likely increase and the population will grow. Now think about conditions in which some resources are scarce. Under conditions of scarce resources, not all organisms can get the resources they need. Fewer organisms are able to reproduce and the population does not grow. If resources are very scarce, some individuals may not survive. Other organisms may reproduce at such a low rate that the population gets smaller. If the amount of resources changes, a population may become larger or smaller.

### Population Size and Resource Availability

Explore the relationship between resource availability and population size on the graph below.

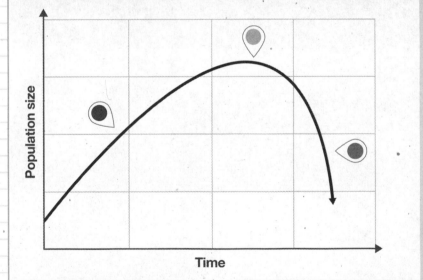

Here, resources are abundant and the population size is increasing.

Here, the population has grown to a maximum size, which cannot be sustained by the amount of resources.

Here, the ecosystem does not have enough resources to support all individuals, so the population size is decreasing.

5. A decrease in a population's rate of reproduction can cause a decrease in population size, such as the one shown on this graph. Which factors might cause a decrease in the rate of reproduction? Select all that apply.

   A. a decrease in the availability of food resources

   B. an increase in resources such as water

   C. conditions that limit the availability of shelter resources

   D. conditions that allow access to new resources that were not previously available

# Factors That Influence Resource Availability

Resource availability influences the growth and survival of individual organisms as well as the sizes of populations. In fact, the types of resources that individuals need are also critical for the population as a whole. Resource availability depends on a variety of factors.

Individuals within a population share the same resources. These individuals may compete with each other for access to these resources. An increase in population size may mean that fewer resources are available for each individual of the population. Different populations of organisms may also share resources, such as water or food. Competition between different populations may result in fewer resources for some populations or individuals.

Environmental factors can also affect resource availability. For example, after a rainy season, plants may produce many leaves and seeds. This large amount of food may allow a deer population to grow. However, when the rain stops and plants produce less, the deer population may decrease. Natural events, such as wildfires and droughts, can limit resource availability temporarily, leading to population decreases.

## Resources in a River Ecosystem

The Alligator Rivers region in Australia is home to a great diversity of wildlife, including the plants, birds, and crocodile seen here. Different bird populations, such as these egrets and storks, share certain resources, including water, nest materials, and fish to eat.

**6.** What factors might affect the availability of fish to eat for the egret and stork populations?

**7.** A red-tailed hawk is a bird that eats other birds and small animals including mammals. Label each scenario to tell whether it would likely increase or decrease the availability of food resources for a red-tailed hawk population.

| Scenario | Effect on red-tailed hawk food resources |
|---|---|
| A drought causes plants to produce fewer seeds than usual, limiting food resources for small mammals. | |
| A disease causes decreases in the populations of mice, voles, ground squirrels, and other small mammals. | |
| Corn crops left in the field provide abundant food for mice and other small mammals. | |

**EVIDENCE NOTEBOOK**

**8.** Think about the organisms that live in a forest. What resources do they need for survival? Record your evidence.

**Engineer It**
# Control Population Growth

Mosquitoes can feed off of the blood of almost any animal, including humans. Their bites can be very unpleasant. They can also transmit a variety of serious diseases. Because of these problems, global efforts exist to design solutions to help limit the sizes of mosquito populations. Mosquitoes require standing water, such as ponds or puddles, to reproduce because their larvae live in these types of water environments.

**9.** Suppose you are tasked with decreasing the mosquito population in a large city with many people. A decrease in which resource would be most effective in decreasing the mosquito population?

**A.** food resources

**B.** water resources

**C.** plant resources

**D.** sunlight resources

**10. Discuss** Brainstorm actions that might limit the availability of this resource for mosquitoes in the area. How might other species be impacted by this change?

_____

_____

_____

# Predicting Effects of Limited Resources

Resources in an ecosystem are often limited, so individuals must compete for the existing resources to meet their needs. *Competition* occurs when two or more individuals or populations try to use the same limited resource.

Competition can happen among individuals within a population. For example, deer in a forest compete with each other for the same plants to eat. This competition increases in winter when many plants die. If an organism does not get the resources it needs, it may not survive to reproduce. Competition also happens among populations. For example, different species of trees in a forest compete with each other for sunlight, water, and space.

Turtles sun themselves to warm their bodies. These turtles are competing for a sunny spot on this rock.

Some bird species only nest in forested areas that are large and continuous.

Human activities can divide large forests into smaller parts. This means some birds may not find nesting sites.

11. Which of the following is most likely to happen when birds cannot find nesting sites as seen in the image above?

   A. The birds wait until a tree becomes available for nesting.

   B. The birds move to another area with more shelter resources.

   C. The birds build a different kind of shelter instead of a nest.

12. **Write** Think about the birds that are left without nesting sites. Write a short story from the point of view of one of those birds. In your story, describe the types of resources you depend on for survival, a situation that led to the lack of resources, and how you responded to the lack of resources.

**Hands-On Lab**
# Investigate Effects of Limited Resources

You will plan and conduct an investigation of how a specific resource can limit the growth of bean plants. Resources and other factors that affect the growth and health of living things are called *limiting factors*.

**MATERIALS**
- cups with sprouted bean plants, 8 oz (4)
- marker
- ruler
- water

## Procedure and Analysis

**STEP 1** Gather your materials. With your group, choose to investigate water or sunlight as a limiting factor.

**STEP 2** Make a hypothesis related to the limiting factor and the bean plants.

**STEP 3** Plan a two-week investigation to test your hypothesis. On a separate sheet of paper, describe the steps of your procedure. Your procedure should identify the variables and controls of the investigation, the types of data that you will collect, and how you will record the data.

**STEP 4** Have your teacher approve your procedure. Revise as necessary.

**STEP 5** Set up your experiment according to your procedure.

**STEP 6** On a separate sheet of paper, make a data table and record data according to your plan.

**STEP 7** Did your data support your hypothesis?

**STEP 8** Make a claim about how the limiting factor you chose affects bean plants. Use your data as evidence to support your claim and explain your reasoning.

**STEP 9** How could you improve your procedure to obtain clearer results?

# Limited Abiotic Resources

Abiotic factors are the nonliving parts of an ecosystem, such as air, water, nutrients, soil, sunlight, and rainfall. Individuals of a population depend on an ecosystem's abiotic resources for survival. For example, the amount of oxygen dissolved in lake water is an important abiotic resource for fish that live in the lake. If there is plenty of oxygen and other resources that fish need, fish will be healthy and fish populations may increase in size. But if oxygen becomes limited, the health of individual fish may suffer, and fish populations may decline.

## Rain Forest Ecosystem

13. **Draw**  The availability of light varies at different elevations in a rain forest. Use a pencil to shade the band to the right of the drawing—darkest where the forest receives the least amount of light and lightest where it receives the most light.

14. Explain where light is likely a limiting factor in this rain forest. What factors do you think are limited at other levels in the forest?

# Limited Biotic Resources

Biotic factors are the parts of an ecosystem that are living or are related to the activity of living things. Bacteria, algae, fungi, plants, and animals are all biotic factors. Decaying organisms are also considered biotic factors. Biotic resources can also become limited. For example, suppose that a fungus destroys the fruits of a tree on which a certain kind of insect feeds. The insect population will decrease because less food is available to individuals. In turn, other animals that feed on the insect will also have less food. The decrease in food would continue to the top of the food chain. An ecosystem's biotic factors are interconnected, so limits to any single factor can affect all other factors.

**15.** Draw a line to connect each change in resource availability with its effect.

| Change in Resources | Effects |
|---|---|
| A region experiences drought conditions for several years. | Population size decreases as individuals compete for access to food resources. |
| A disease greatly decreases the size of a population of woodpeckers. | Mates become harder to find. |
| A population of fish greatly increases in size after a short-term increase in food availability. | Plant growth is greatly limited. |

 **EVIDENCE NOTEBOOK**

**16.** Wildfires not only burn down trees and other plants, they can also burn much of the materials and nutrients in the top layer of soil. Think about the abiotic and biotic resources that may become limited after a wildfire. How would individual organisms and populations be affected? Record your evidence.

# Predict Effects on a Population

Lions and hyenas—like the ones in the photo—live in similar habitats in a number of African ecosystems. Lions and hyenas rely on the same food resources.

Populations of lions and hyenas compete for the same food resources.

**17.** Predict how an increase in the hyena population would affect the population of lions. Then think of a similar interaction in a different ecosystem. Predict how an increase in one population from your example would affect the other population.

_____

_____

_____

_____

_____

# Predicting Effects of Abundant Resources

Some resources are abundant in certain ecosystems. An example is sunlight, which is usually an abundant resource on the prairie. In other cases, resources may become abundant for a short time. For example, some species of insects, known as periodical cicadas, have 13- or 17-year life cycles. Every 13 or 17 years, large numbers of these cicadas emerge after developing underground. Birds and many other animals eat these types of cicadas. When the cicadas emerge, they produce an incredible abundance of food resources for their predators.

The photos below show an example of resource abundance caused by humans. Rainwater runoff carries garden and agricultural fertilizers into aquatic ecosystems. The abundant nutrients cause extreme growth of algal populations, called an *algal bloom*.

## Algal Bloom Caused by Nutrient Abundance

The aerial photographs show a body of water with a typical amount of nutrients and a body of water during an algal bloom. During an algal bloom, nutrient resources that were once limited became abundant, allowing the algal populations to grow.

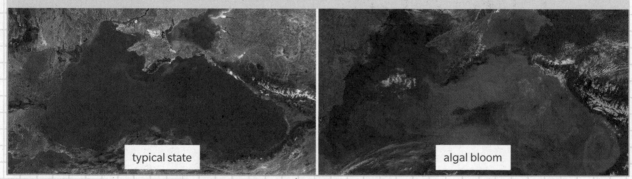

typical state

algal bloom

18. **Discuss**  If the algae in an algal bloom never run out of nutrients, what other factor do you think might limit their population growth?

## Abundant Abiotic and Biotic Resources

An abundance of abiotic or biotic resources can result in the growth of individuals and populations. An abundance of food, which is a biotic factor, can specifically lead to population growth. However, an excess of certain resources can sometimes limit growth. For example, a plant that thrives in shaded areas may not survive in direct sunlight.

19. Weeks of rainfall have provided an abundance of water resources in a region that is usually not so wet. Which of the following are likely effects of the abundance of water? Select all that apply.

  A. Some plants may thrive.

  B. Some plants may be washed away.

  C. Some plants may have limited growth.

### Do the Math
# Analyze Population Growth Data

If resources are abundant, a population may grow at an increasing rate. When the population size increases by a factor repeatedly, the growth is called *exponential growth*.

**Alaskan Reindeer Population Size**

This graph shows changes in the Alaskan reindeer population between 1910 and 1950, which includes a period of exponential growth.

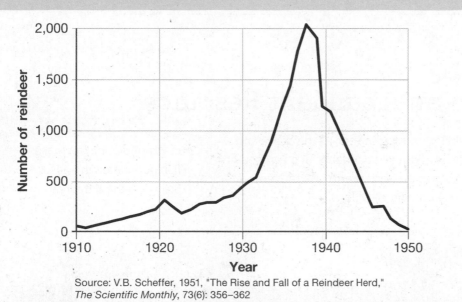

Source: V.B. Scheffer, 1951, "The Rise and Fall of a Reindeer Herd," *The Scientific Monthly*, 73(6): 356–362

**20.** What was the largest reindeer population size during the years shown in the graph? Round your answer to the nearest hundred.

**21.** During which years did the reindeer population experience exponential growth? Explain your answer.

**22.** Analyze the data shown in the graph. Form an argument for why a large decrease in the reindeer population size occurred following the period of exponential population growth.

**23.** Draw a line to connect each change in resource availability with its effect.

| Change in Resources | Effects |
|---|---|
| Resource availability remains steady. | Population size decreases. |
| Availability of resources becomes more limited. | Population size increases. |
| Resources become abundant for a period of time. | Population size remains the same. |

**Language SmArts**

# Analyze an Abundant Resource

**24.** The diagram shows the relationship between a type of fish and crabs that the fish eat. How might an abundance of one resource affect the other populations in the ecosystem? Use the terms in the box to label the cause-and-effect diagram.

- crab population decreases
- fish population increases
- fish population decreases

crab population increases

# Continue Your Exploration

**Name:** _____     **Date:** _____

**Check out the path below or go online to choose one of the other paths shown.**

Analyzing Types of Population Growth

- Hands-On Labs 🖑
- Monarch Butterfly Survival
- Propose Your Own Path

*Go online to choose one of these other paths.*

Population growth is often represented by two different models: an exponential growth model and a logistic growth model. *Exponential growth* occurs when resource abundance allows for a continued increase in the growth rate of a population. In *logistic growth,* the rate of population growth slows as the population approaches a maximum size. Logistic growth occurs because one or more resources limit the growth of the population. When a population has reached the maximum size that can be sustained by available resources, the population size levels off.

The population growth of these harbor seals exhibits a logistic growth pattern because their population size is limited by competition for resources and predation.

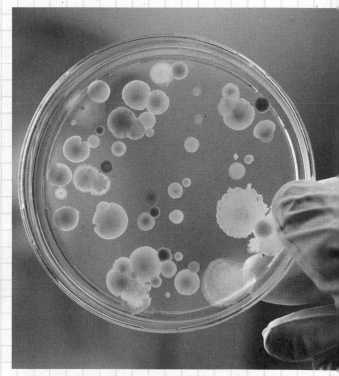

In a Petri dish with plenty of nutrients and space, these bacteria exhibit an exponential growth pattern until resources become limited.

© Houghton Mifflin Harcourt • Image Credits: (l) ©James Warwick/Oxford Scientific/Getty Images; (r) ©AndreasReh/Vetta/Getty Images

# Continue Your Exploration

1. In both growth models, population growth occurs when resources are
   abundant / limited.. Exponential / Logistic growth continues to
   increase while resources are abundant, while exponential / logistic growth
   slows down due to limits in resource availability.

2. What is the greatest difference between the two growth models? Explain your answer.

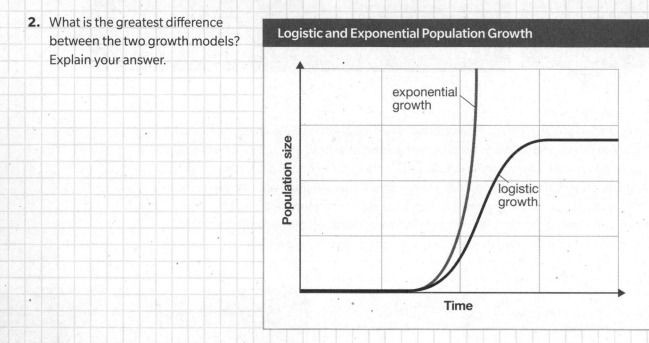

**Logistic and Exponential Population Growth**

3. Which population growth model do you think best describes most populations in an ecosystem? Justify your response.

4. **Collaborate** Research another species that experiences logistic growth and another species that experiences exponential growth. For each example, describe a key resource that affects population size, and describe the availability of that resource. Prepare a presentation to share with your class that explains each example.

# Can You Explain It?

Name: _____ Date: _____

### How does a wildfire affect resources and populations in a forest?

*Explore ONLINE!*

**EVIDENCE NOTEBOOK**

Refer to the notes in your Evidence Notebook to help you construct an explanation for how a wildfire affects resources and populations in a forest ecosystem.

1. State your claim. Make sure your claim fully explains how a wildfire affects resources and populations in a forest ecosystem.

2. Summarize the evidence you have gathered to support your claim and explain your reasoning.

# Checkpoints

**Answer the following questions to check your understanding of the lesson.**

**Use the information in the table to answer Questions 3–4.**

3. Which of the resources listed would organisms most likely compete over in the abyssal zone?

   **A.** shelter

   **B.** sunlight

   **C.** nutrients

   **D.** temperature

| Resource Availability in Three Marine Habitats | | | |
|---|---|---|---|
| **Resource** | **Habitat 1: Coral reef** | **Habitat 2: Mesopelagic zone** | **Habitat 3: Abyssal zone** |
| sunlight | high | low | none |
| temperature | warm | moderate | cold |
| shelter | medium | none | none |
| nutrients | high | medium | low |

4. The most diverse community would typically be found in the

   coral reef / mesopelagic zone / abyssal zone because it has the

   least / greatest amount of basic resources.

---

**Use the caribou photo to answer Questions 5–6.**

5. How might an abundance of food resources affect the caribou population? Select all that apply.

   **A.** The population would increase in size.

   **B.** The population would decrease in size.

   **C.** The caribou would start to eat other types of food.

   **D.** There would be less competition between the caribou for food.

6. How would a shortage of water likely affect the caribou? Select all that apply.

   **A.** The population would increase in size.

   **B.** The population would decrease in size.

   **C.** The growth of individual caribou would increase.

   **D.** The growth of individual caribou would decrease.

# Interactive Review

**Complete this section to review the main concepts of the lesson.**

The growth of individuals and populations depends on resource availability.

**A.** What basic resources do organisms and populations need to grow?

Biotic and abiotic factors can limit population growth.

**B.** Describe one biotic factor and one abiotic factor that can limit population growth.

Resource abundance can promote population growth.

**C.** Explain the relationship between resource availability and population growth.

Getty Images

# Patterns of Interaction

These fish enjoy a feast of algae on the sea turtle's shell. It is an easy meal compared to foraging among ocean plants or reefs.

**By the end of this lesson . . .**

you will be able to explain patterns of interaction between organisms.

© Houghton Mifflin Harcourt • Image Credits: ©WaterFrame/Alamy

# CAN YOU EXPLAIN IT?

**How could a devastating drought lead to a population increase of coyotes?**

Surface waters in California gradually shrink during a long drought. All ecosystem populations are deprived of a needed resource. Resourceful coyotes found ways to adjust to the new environmental conditions.

1. Think about what happens to an ecosystem's plant and animal life during a drought. Suggest possible impacts to a plant, a freshwater fish, and a rabbit.

2. What ecosystem changes might lead to an increase in the population of a predator, such as a coyote? Consider the changes to both living and nonliving resources in the ecosystem.

**EVIDENCE NOTEBOOK** As you explore the lesson, gather evidence to explain how a severe drought could cause an increase in a coyote population.

# Analyzing Feeding Relationships

Think about all the ways you are connected to other organisms. Both plants and animals provide you with resources that you need. You may eat meat from a variety of animals. You get food and fiber from plants. You also provide resources to some animals, such as the blood a mosquito gets when it bites you. Another way you are connected with other animals is through social interactions. For example, you laugh with your friends or play fetch with your dog.

Feeding interactions and relationships are some of the most important connections between organisms. Without the energy and nutrients provided by food, organisms would starve. Plants make their own food. But animals must eat other organisms to get the energy and nutrients they need. Some animals eat plants, some eat other animals, and some eat both.

3. **Discuss** Together with a partner, compare the feeding habits of the animals in the photos. Which animal has the most diverse diet? Which animal has the least diverse diet? Discuss two advantages of each feeding strategy.

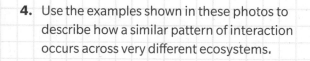

4. Use the examples shown in these photos to describe how a similar pattern of interaction occurs across very different ecosystems.

A koala's diet consists almost solely of eucalyptus leaves. Koalas are one of three organisms in the world that can feed on eucalyptus leaves, which are low in nutrients and contain many toxins.

Lions feed only on meaty animals of the savanna, such as zebra or gazelle. They may catch prey from the large herds that graze near watering holes.

The pink color of flamingos' feathers comes from red pigments in their food, which includes red algae and shrimp. They also eat aquatic plants, insects, and small fish.

## Predators Eat Prey

With its toothless duck-like bill, webbed feet, and cat-sized furry body, you might be surprised to learn that the platypus is a feisty predator. A **predator** is an animal that captures and eats other animals. The platypus is a *carnivore*, an organism that feeds exclusively on animal flesh. Its **prey,** or hunted food source, includes shellfish, worms, insects, and fish larvae. Most carnivores have sharp teeth to hold or rip their prey. But platypuses use gravel scooped up with their water-dwelling prey to grind food into small pieces. As with other carnivores, the number of platypuses in an area depends on the availability of prey. Factors that limit prey will also, in turn, limit platypuses.

The platypus is sticking its bill in the bottom of the stream in search of the animals that it eats.

A spider wraps an insect tightly with silk threads.

5. Using evidence from the photo, describe the interaction between the spider and the insect. How do the two images support the idea that predatory interactions occur in different ecosystems?

## Herbivores Eat Plants or Algae

Unlike carnivores, some organisms get energy and nutrients from plants or algae. These organisms are called **herbivores.** Some herbivores feed only on the leaves of particular plants. Others take advantage of a range of plant parts. The mountain gorilla, for example, feeds on the leaves and shoots of trees. The monarch butterfly feeds on milkweed leaves as a caterpillar and on nectar from flowers as a winged adult.

Algae are unicellular or multicellular organisms that can make their own food through photosynthesis. Algae live in water ecosystems, where they collect light energy from sunlight. They provide food for large numbers of herbivores. Kelp is a type of algae that can grow to be more than 50 m in length. Crabs and many other shellfish eat kelp. These animals are food for carnivores, such as the red octopus.

© Houghton Mifflin Harcourt • Image Credits: (t) ©Marie Read/Science Source; (c) ©Jarp2/Shutterstock; (b) ©Brian J. Skerry/National Geographic/Getty Images

Manatees are herbivores. These manatees are feeding on lettuce and other plants in a natural spring in Homosassa, Florida.

# Hands-On Lab
# Simulate Feeding Relationships

Simulate the interactions among plants, herbivores, and omnivores over several seasons. Use graphical evidence to analyze patterns of change in clover, rabbit, and coyote populations as they experience typical seasonal weather interrupted by unexpected events.

Carnivores consume animals and herbivores only eat plants or algae. *Omnivores* are organisms that consume both plants and animals. In this simulation, coyotes eat rabbits. However, in a real ecosystem, they are omnivores and eat a variety of plants and animals.

**MATERIALS**
- beans, red kidney (coyotes)
- beans, white navy (rabbits)
- graph paper
- peas, split green (clover)
- pencils, colored
- penny
- ruler

### Cottontail
*Sylvilagus floridanus*

### Attributes
*Shy, Evasive, Adaptable, and Quick*

**Type:** Mammal
**Diet:** Herbivore
**Habitat:** Fields and Meadows
**Average Life Span:** Less than 3 years
**Size:** 39.5 to 47.7 cm
**Weight:** 800 to 1533 g

### Red Clover
*Trifolium pratense*

### Attributes
*Drought Resistant, Edible, Nonnative*

**Type:** Perennial
**Growth:** Short-lived, highly productive
**Habitat:** Fields and Meadows
**Stem:** hollow stems, 60 to 80 cm
**Leaf:** Palmately trifoliate, variegated
**Flower:** rose, purple, or magenta

### Coyote
*Canis latrans*

### Attributes
*Clever, Sneaky, Adaptable, and Swims*

**Type:** Mammal
**Diet:** Omnivore
**Habitat:** Prefers Fields and Prairies
**Average Life Span:** Up to 14 years
**Size:** Head and body, 81 to 94 cm; Tail, 41 cm
**Weight:** 9 to 23 kg

## Procedure

**STEP 1** Place beans that represent 20 clover plants, 12 rabbits, and 6 coyotes on your table. This models a stable community during the winter.

**STEP 2** Using the sample below, create a line graph on graph paper to track population sizes over four seasons. Choose a different colored pencil for each type of organism. Then plot each starting population number for the winter on your graph. Continue to plot the size of each population as you complete Step 3.

Population size — Winter — Spring — Summer — Fall

**STEP 3** Use the instructions in the table to model seasonal population changes. Follow these guidelines:

- For each season, add or remove beans according to the information in the *Seasonal Changes* column.
- Then flip a coin to complete either the heads (H) or tails (T) directions for that season.
- Remove beans for organisms that die. Add beans for births, new growth, or organisms that migrate into the area.
- Recount each type of bean. As you finish each season, plot the end-of-season population on your graph.
- If a population reaches zero organisms, it exits the simulation.

| Seasonal Changes | Coin Flip |
|---|---|
| **Spring**<br>The clover population doubles. Each rabbit eats 2 clover plants. Each coyote eats 1 rabbit. | **H:** Heavy rains cause 15 more clover plants to grow. For every 2 rabbits, 5 more are born, but 2 coyotes die from disease.<br>**T:** For every 2 rabbits, 6 more are born. Construction forces 3 more coyotes to join the population. |
| **Summer**<br>The clover population triples. Each rabbit eats 2 clover plants. Each coyote eats 1 rabbit. | **H:** Drought wipes out half the clover population. For every 2 rabbits only 2 rabbits are born. One coyote dies from dehydration.<br>**T:** Late rains allow 10 new clover plants to grow. For every 2 rabbits, 6 new rabbits are born. |
| **Fall**<br>The clover population doubles. Each rabbit eats 2 clover plants. Each coyote eats 1 rabbit. | **H:** Over-grazing kills half the clover population. Five rabbits die for lack of food. Two coyotes also die of starvation.<br>**T:** A warm fall spurs growth of 9 new clover plants and a longer breeding season for rabbits. For every 2 rabbits, 4 more rabbits are born. |

**STEP 4** Connect the population plots on your graph to show the changes in population size for each organism. Remember to use a different color for each type of organism.

## Analysis

**STEP 5** Which populations were the most strongly affected by seasonal changes? Include evidence to support your argument.

**STEP 6** Look at your graph to analyze how changes to one population affect changes to other populations. Using your data, predict how the following winter might affect the three populations in this activity. Explain your reasoning.

# Relationships Between Population Sizes

When mice begin to invade grain storehouses, farmers may bring a few cats to their farm. Elsewhere, conservationists work to increase impala populations so that endangered cheetahs have plenty of food to raise healthy cubs. These farmers and conservationists understand that populations of carnivores and herbivores are related. If one population in a feeding relationship increases or decreases, the other population is affected.

**EVIDENCE NOTEBOOK**

6. What does a population of coyotes need in order to increase in size? How might a drought help to fulfill the need? Record your evidence.

**Do the Math**

# Analyze Relationships

Graphs of population size are one tool used to identify patterns in ecosystem interactions. Some scientists closely follow the interactions between moose and wolf populations. As predators and prey, these animals are closely linked. Analyzing moose and wolf population data helps scientists understand their relationship.

7. Analyze the graph to determine the changes that are happening near A, B, and C. Write the letter next to the statement that describes the relationship between each population change.

_____ Both populations are increasing.

_____ Wolf populations are decreasing.

_____ More wolves are eating moose.

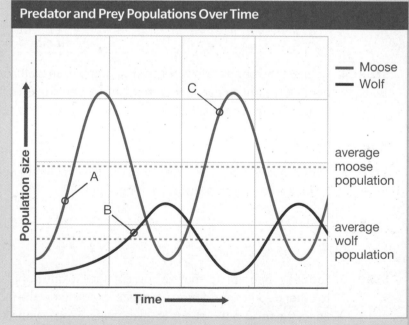

8. In the graph showing moose and wolf populations over time, 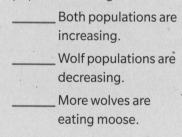 time / population size is the dependent variable. The independent variable is time / population size.

9. Describe how the dependent and independent variables help explain the feeding relationship between moose and wolves.

_____

_____

_____

_____

# Explaining Symbiotic Relationships

Some species within an ecosystem interact very closely. For example, clownfish live in anemones, birds nest in trees, and humans and dogs have loyal relationships. One species may depend completely on another for survival. Without the hardworking actions of the fig wasp, for example, fig trees could not reproduce. Fig trees produce flowers. But these flowers are all grouped together inside a structure that has a tough skin. This structure is often referred to as the fig's "fruit." Only tiny fig wasps will bore into the fruit, pollinating the figs as they feed.

Clownfish make their home within the stinging tentacles of sea anemones. The clownfish is not harmed by the anemone, but potential predators can be. The darting clownfish bring a rush of fresh ocean water to the anemone. This water clears away the nutrient-depleted water trapped between its tentacles.

10. How does the interaction between clownfish and anemones benefit each species? Cite your evidence next to each photo below.

clownfish

anemone

## Symbiotic Relationships

As scientists study ecosystems, they observe patterns in the strategies organisms use to survive and reproduce within a community. Many of these patterns include symbiotic relationships. **Symbiosis** refers to the close, long-term relationship between two species within an ecosystem. Many symbiotic relationships help organisms get important nonliving resources from the environment. For example, animals gain nitrogen for making proteins from their food. But plants also need a source of nitrogen. Bacteria living in the roots of many plants provide nitrogen. In turn, the plant roots provide energy-rich sugars to the bacteria.

There are three types of symbiotic relationships. They are categorized based on whether each organism benefits, is harmed, or is unaffected by the relationship.

**11.** After reading about the interactions in the photos below, write whether each organism benefits, is not affected, or is harmed in the space provided.

The tick lives in the dog's fur and feeds off the dog's blood. As it feeds, the tick exposes the dog to microorganisms through the transfer of blood.

Remora fish follow or attach themselves through suction to the whale shark. Remoras feed on leftovers from the shark's meals.

Pollen from the flower sticks to the bee as it drinks nectar. While visiting the flower, the bee may transfer pollen from another flower. As a result of pollination, the plant can reproduce.

**A.** The dog _____ by the interaction, while the tick _____ .

**B.** The remora _____ by the interaction, while the whale shark _____ .

**C.** The bee _____ by the interaction, while the flower _____ .

## Mutualism

Mutualism occurs when both organisms benefit from an interaction. These relationships usually occur between species that do not compete with each other, but there are exceptions. For example, zebra and wildebeest each feed on the wild grasses of the savanna. Yet, they migrate together in large numbers across the Serengeti plains in Kenya each year. By doing so, they deter predators such as lions or cheetahs. Some mutualistic interactions are so close that they involve one organism hosting another within its body. *Trichonympha (trik•uh•NIM•fuh)* are unicellular organisms that live within the intestines of termites. They gain energy and a safe home while helping termites break down hard-to-digest wood.

## Commensalism

In commensalism, one organism benefits from an interaction, and the other is unaffected. For example, antbirds in tropical forests follow behind army ants. They eat small insects driven from plant leaves by the stampeding ants. High above the ground, certain bromeliad plants wrap tough roots around the upper branches of rain forest trees to get enough sunlight. The ants, trees, and snails are unaffected by these interactions. Organisms that benefit from commensalism are able to take better advantage of environmental resources.

# Parasitism

Predators kill and eat their prey, but parasites may feed on host organisms without killing them. While the parasite benefits from this interaction, the host is harmed. Fleas, ticks, and leeches are examples of parasites that feed on the blood of their animal hosts. These parasites attach to the hosts. Some parasites enter the host's body to obtain what they need. Tapeworms live within the intestines of some animals. They eat from their host's undigested food. As a result, fewer nutrients are left for the host.

12. What type of symbiotic relationship does the dodder plant have with the host plant? Which plant benefits from this interaction?

   **A.** mutualism; the dodder plant benefits

   **B.** predation; the host plant benefits

   **C.** commensalism; the dodder plant benefits

   **D.** parasitism; the dodder plant benefits

13. **Act** Pair with another student to act out a symbiotic relationship while your classmates guess the type of interaction.

   **a.** Record a brief description of the different symbiotic interactions presented.

   **b.** Explain how your presentation to the class modeled a pattern of symbiosis.

This dodder plant has no chlorophyll. It winds its stems around another plant. Then the dodder sends rootlike organs into the host plant's tissues to steal food.

## Predict Population Changes

14. In the dark depths of the ocean, a female anglerfish extends a glowing ball from a modified spine to lure prey. The glow comes from symbiotic bacteria that give off light from certain chemical reactions. The anglerfish "lure" provides the bacteria with nutrients and a place to live. This provides evidence for what type of interaction? Explain what might happen to the anglerfish and bacteria populations if this relationship did not occur.

   _____

   _____

   _____

   _____

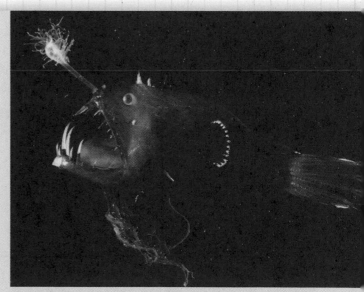

The anglerfish attracts prey by "fishing" with a lure protruding from a spine near the top of its mouth. Only female anglerfish have lures to attract prey.

   _____

   _____

   _____

   _____

# Predicting Effects of Competitive Interactions

Athletes train for years to compete against the best of the best at the Olympic games. Each athlete uses a large amount of resources to compete, including time, energy, and money. Only one athlete wins each event in the end. However, competition encourages all athletes to build on their strengths and reduce their weaknesses over time. Competition for limited resources among populations also involves costs and benefits.

15. **Discuss** Working with a partner, brainstorm a list of resources that populations might compete for in an ecosystem. Choose one resource from your list to consider further. What evidence might you gather to determine whether two populations compete for this resource?

## Competition for Resources

Organisms with similar needs tend to compete for resources. All plants, for example, require sunlight. The tallest trees in a rain forest create a canopy that blocks sun. Therefore, plants below must compete for the limited light passing through the leaves of taller trees. Some plants have adaptations that help them gather light. They compete effectively and build a stable population size. Liana vines, for example, may grow as long as 915 m to reach sunlight available at the rain forest canopy.

The interactions that occur between organisms when they both seek the same resource in an ecosystem are called **competition**. Each organism or population gets less of the resource than it would if there were no competitors. For example, in dry environments, many types of organisms compete for limited water resources.

Water is a limited resource in the Namib Desert in Africa. These zebras and hartebeest compete for access to the same watering hole.

© Houghton Mifflin Harcourt • Image Credits: ©Jami Tarris/Corbis Documentary/Getty Images

**16.** Use what you have learned about competition to complete the cause-and-effect table.

| Cause | Effect |
|---|---|
| A population of lions grows too large to share their current territory. | |
| | Several male hyenas compete to mate with the females present in their area. |
| | Lions, leopards, and cheetahs compete for zebras to eat. |
| Zebras and wildebeests both feed on savanna grasses. Recent heavy rains have caused the grass population to flourish. | |

**Language SmArts**

# Explain Evidence of Competition

The green anole lizard is native to southern Florida. The anoles climb trees to hunt insects and return to the ground to lay eggs. Sightings of green anoles have been declining over the last two decades. A species of brown anole from Cuba seems to be taking over the area. They are effective hunters. Researchers observe that as brown anoles continue to move in, green anoles shift their activities higher in trees.

green anole

brown anole

**Habitat:** They are native to the southeastern United States, prefer bushes and trees, and may climb up to canopy level.
**Diet:** They eat insects, spiders, and flies.
**Predators:** They are eaten by skinks, snakes, birds, and other lizards.

**Habitat:** They are native to Cuba and the Bahamas, are mainly ground dwelling, and may climb up to 1.5 m.
**Diet:** They eat insects, spiders, worms, snails, slugs, and other small reptiles (including hatchling green anoles).
**Predators:** They are eaten by skinks, snakes, and birds.

**17.** Brown anoles eat adult / the same prey as green anoles. The two anole types are competitors. Additional evidence of competition includes displaying behaviors to defend territory by both anole types, as well as how brown anoles / green anoles move higher into trees to find prey.

**18.** Look again at the pattern of population growth for wolves and moose presented in the graph. If grizzly bears, which also feed on moose, are introduced to the same ecosystem, how might the graph change?

**Predator and Prey Populations over Time**

 **EVIDENCE NOTEBOOK**

**19.** Explain how a drought might change a coyote's normal feeding habits. What effect could the change have on competition? Record your evidence.

 **Engineer It**

# Use Competition to Control Population Size

A nonnative fish is causing trouble in the Mississippi River. Asian carp came to the United States from China in the ballast water of ships. The carp reproduce in large numbers and eat large amounts of plankton. They also increase water cloudiness by eating shoreline plants and jump easily over barriers made to control their migration. Populations of native mussels and small fish that also feed on plankton are in decline. Larger fish species also suffer because their prey populations have decreased and their shoreline nurseries have been destroyed. As carp numbers rise, ecologists seek solutions.

**20.** Which of the following methods would cause competition for resources among carp and therefore help control the carp population?

**A.** Ecologists sprout plants distasteful to carp along unvegetated river shoreline.

**B.** Thousands of mussels are relocated from the Great Lakes to the Mississippi River.

**C.** State officials offer free licenses to fishermen that catch more than 100 Asian carp each year.

**D.** Conservationists build protective fences around grasses where native plankton-eating fish lay their eggs.

# Continue Your Exploration

**Name:**                                            **Date:**

**Check out the path below or go online to choose one of the other paths shown.**

**Environmental Changes and Interactions**

- **Hands-On Labs** 🖐
- **Cleaning Symbiosis**
- **Propose Your Own Path**

*Go online to choose one of these other paths.*

Large-scale changes in environmental conditions can change patterns of interaction in ecosystems. During El Niño weather cycles, for example, global winds and ocean currents shift. These shifts cause changes to ecosystems around the world. In 2016, an intense El Niño cycle caused severe droughts in Zimbabwe. Crops and livestock populations there decreased rapidly. As a result, competition for food increased among human groups. Half a world away, the same El Niño cycle caused flooding in Paraguay. Mosquito populations flourished. Viral diseases in humans that are transmitted by mosquitoes, such as dengue, spread.

    El Niño cycles have natural causes and are temporary. However, human influences on the environment can last a very long time. For example, the use of fossil fuels can lead to ocean warming, a difficult trend to reverse. Warmer waters draw tiger sharks from their normal feeding grounds along tropical coasts into northern waters and the open ocean. As they move to new territories, sharks affect the interactions among organisms.

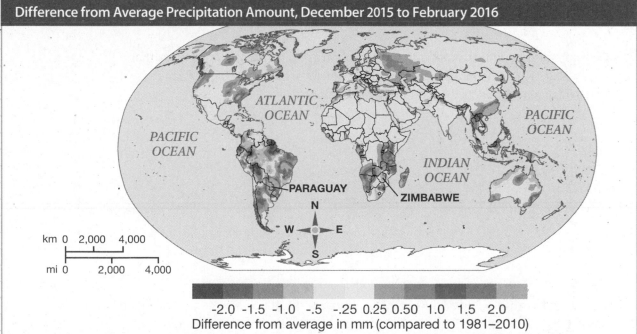

**Difference from Average Precipitation Amount, December 2015 to February 2016**

-2.0 -1.5 -1.0 -.5 -.25 0.25 0.50 1.0 1.5 2.0
Difference from average in mm (compared to 1981–2010)

*Source:* E. Becker, 2016, "March 2016 El Niño update: Spring Forward," with data from the Climate Prediction Center, ENSO Blog, Climate.gov

© Houghton Mifflin Harcourt

# Continue Your Exploration

1. How will warmer ocean temperatures likely affect the competitive interactions of tiger sharks? Explain what might happen to the size of shark and competitor populations.

As apex predators, tiger sharks consume many types of ocean prey.

2. As humans burn fossil fuels, the amount of carbon dioxide in the air and ocean increases. Reefs are declining as ocean carbon dioxide depletes resources used by coral to build skeletons. Other factors, including nutrient pollution and increasing ocean temperatures, are also linked to reef decline. Predict what will happen to populations that have mutualistic, commensal, and parasitic interactions with the coral.

3. Compare the changes that occur to an ecosystem as a result of El Niño to those that are a result of human influence on the ecosystem. Relate the scale of the changes, and explain how it affects the patterns of interaction.

4. **Collaborate** An *infographic* is a colorful, one-page resource that presents information using symbols more than words. With a group, design an example-filled infographic explaining how environmental changes can affect symbiotic and competitive interactions. Topics could include the relationships between the oxpecker bird and a zebra, an orca and a seal, or a mosquito and a deer.

© Houghton Mifflin Harcourt • Image Credits: ©Alastair Pollock Photography/Moment/ Getty Images

# Can You Explain It?

Name: _____  Date: _____

How could a devastating drought lead to a population increase of coyotes?

### EVIDENCE NOTEBOOK

Refer to the notes in your Evidence Notebook to help you construct an explanation for how a coyote population might increase during a drought.

1.  State your argument. Make sure your claims fully explain the role of feeding relationships and community interactions in the increase of the coyote population during a drought.

2.  Summarize the evidence you have gathered to support your claim and explain your reasoning.

# Checkpoints

Answer the following questions to check your understanding of the lesson.

Use the photo to answer Questions 3–4.

3. Which statements describe the feeding interaction between frogs and insects? Circle all that apply.

   A. The frog is a predator.

   B. The interaction is mutualistic.

   C. The frog is a parasite.

   D. The number of insects can influence the number of frogs in the ecosystem.

4. If a drought causes insect populations to decrease, the frog population will likely increase / decrease / remain stable. If populations of birds that eat insects increase, the frog population will likely increase / decrease / remain stable.

Use the photo to answer Questions 5–6.

5. Hundreds of pounds of barnacles may be attached to the surface of whales at a given time. Unnoticed by the whale, barnacles avoid predators and filter plankton from ocean water while the whales feed. In this interaction, the barnacles benefit / are unaffected / are harmed while the whale is unaffected.

6. Whale lice live on the surface of whales. They are very small, and they feed on whale skin. Which statement best describes the relationship between lice and barnacles?

   A. They have a predator-prey relationship.

   B. They are both whale parasites.

   C. They compete for food resources.

   D. They do not compete for food resources, but may compete for space on a whale.

7. Atlantic salmon migrate to rivers in New England to reproduce and to the coast of Greenland to feed. Which of these scenarios could cause a decrease in salmon populations due to competition? Circle all that apply.

   A. Abundant food resources in Greenland

   B. Limited food resources in Greenland

   C. Increased predation by birds

   D. Limited space for reproduction in New England rivers

# Interactive Review

**Complete this page to review the main concepts of the lesson.**

While plants can make their own food, animals must eat other organisms for survival. Carnivores eat animal prey, while herbivores eat plants or algae.

**A.** Explain how the population sizes of two species in a feeding relationship are linked.

Symbiotic interactions are close, long-term relationships between species. At least one species benefits from the relationship, while the other species may benefit, be harmed, or be unaffected.

**B.** Compare the interactions of predators with prey to the interactions of parasites with host organisms.

Organisms that seek the same limited resources will compete with each other.

**C.** What happens to competition when resources are abundant in an ecosystem? Use an example to explain your answer.

**Choose one of the activities to explore how this unit connects to other topics.**

### ☐ Earth Science Connection

**Cycling of Resources**  Many types of resources are involved in cycles. For example, carbon, water, and nitrogen all cycle through Earth's systems, including the atmosphere, hydrosphere, geosphere, and biosphere. Each of these resources is essential for living things.

Using library and Internet sources, research the parts of one of these cycles. Draw a labeled illustration of how the resource cycles through an ecosystem of your choosing. Include a prediction as to how a change in that cycle would impact the different populations living in the ecosystem.

### ☐ Environmental Science Connection

**Drilling in the Arctic**  Under the snow and ice of the Arctic are millions of gallons of oil. This oil would be very useful to people. However, drilling in the ice can threaten Arctic ecosystems.

Investigate the oil drilling that takes place in the Arctic and research the pipeline that moves the oil from the far north. What might happen to Arctic ecosystems if this pipeline were to leak or break? Research the solutions that have been developed to make these pipelines safe. Make a recommendation for at least one of these solutions to be implemented in the Arctic pipeline, and explain your reasoning.

### ☐ Literature Connection

**The Call of the Wild**  Many ecosystem interactions have been written about in popular fiction, such as Jack London's *Call of the Wild*. Popularizing ecosystem interactions in literature can help to educate people about the threats to certain species and entire ecosystems.

Research popular fiction that focuses on ecosystem interactions, such as the novels *Dances with Wolves*, *Watership Down,* and *King of the Wind: The Story of the Godolphin Arabian*. Summarize the novel in a few paragraphs. Then, select a different ecosystem interaction, and write your own short fiction story about it.

Name: _____          Date: _____

**Complete this review to check your understanding of the unit.**

**Use the photo of the macaws to answer Questions 1–2.**

1. What biotic factors are present in this ecosystem? Select all that apply.

   A. rocks

   B. birds

   C. plants

   D. water

2. What might happen to a population of birds, such as these macaws, if there is an increased amount of food and water?

   A. The macaw population will decrease.

   B. The macaw population will increase.

   C. The macaw population will not change.

   D. Competition among macaws will increase.

---

**Use the graph to answer Questions 3–4.**

3. Sea ice is an example of a living / nonliving factor in the Arctic ecosystem. The overall trend in sea ice cover is that it has increased / decreased / remained the same. Since 1979, the most cover was during 1983 / 1992 / 2009 and the least amount was during 1980 / 1995 / 2012.

4. Walruses use sea ice as a diving platform to feed on clams on the sea floor. What prediction can be made about sea ice cover in the year 2020 and how will it impact walruses?

   A. The ice cover will increase and walrus populations will grow.

   B. The ice cover will continue to decrease and walrus populations will decline.

   C. The ice cover will continue to decrease but walruses will move to new areas and populations will grow.

   D. The ice cover will increase but there will not be enough space for walruses to live.

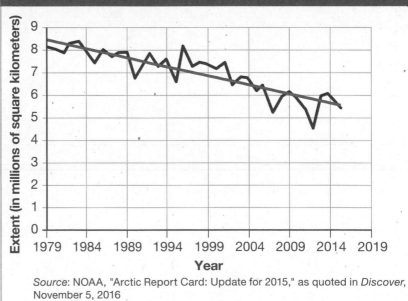

**Average Monthly Arctic Sea Ice Extent**

*Source*: NOAA, "Arctic Report Card: Update for 2015," as quoted in *Discover*, November 5, 2016

**5.** Complete the table by describing patterns related to each type of relationship, as well as the effect of each relationship on individuals and populations.

| Relationships in Ecosystems | Patterns Across Ecosystems | Effects on Individuals | Effects on Populations |
|---|---|---|---|
| Competition for Resources | In any ecosystem, organisms with similar needs for food, water, or other resources may compete with each other when a resource becomes limited. | | |
| Predator-Prey | | | |
| Herbivore-Plant/Algae | | | |
| Mutualism | | | |

**Name:** _____      **Date:** _____

**Use the graph to answer Questions 6–9.**

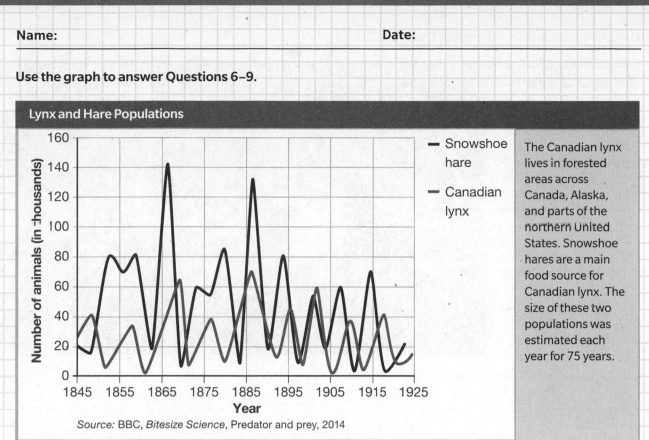

Lynx and Hare Populations

— Snowshoe hare

— Canadian lynx

The Canadian lynx lives in forested areas across Canada, Alaska, and parts of the northern United States. Snowshoe hares are a main food source for Canadian lynx. The size of these two populations was estimated each year for 75 years.

*Source: BBC, Bitesize Science, Predator and prey, 2014*

**6.** Explain the pattern displayed in this graph in terms of the relationship between predator and prey population sizes.

**7.** Snowshoe hares eat grasses, small leafy plants, and flowers. When hare populations peak, these plant food sources can become scarce. What can you conclude about the size of these plant populations from 1910–1915?

**8.** How would decreased availability of plant food sources affect the populations of snowshoe hares? Would competition for food likely increase or decrease?

**9.** Provide different examples of how changes in biotic and abiotic resources could affect the stability of this ecosystem.

**Use the photo and text to answer Questions 10–13.**

### Oxpeckers and Cape Buffalo

This photo shows a cape buffalo and several birds, called oxpeckers, on the African savanna. The oxpecker birds get insects, a main food source, from the buffalo. The buffalo benefits by having insects removed from its fur. However, this relationship can also harm the buffalo. The oxpeckers sometimes open old wounds to feed on the buffalo's blood.

**10.** Explain why this relationship could be considered an example of mutualism.

**11.** Some scientists consider this relationship semi-parasitic. What evidence would suggest that this relationship might be parasitic?

**12.** What might happen if oxpeckers began to eat insects from other sources, instead of from the buffalo? Explain your reasoning.

**13.** How do you think the buffalo population would be affected if the oxpecker population dramatically increased in size? Explain your reasoning.

Name: _____          Date: _____

# How do lionfish affect relationships in local ecosystems?

The red lionfish (*Pterois volitans*) is an invasive species in the Gulf of Mexico. While beautiful, it is also very deadly due to its venomous spines. As an invasive species, it is causing much damage to the native ecosystems. This fish has no natural predators in the area, lays 50,000 eggs every three days, and has a life span of 30 years. Your task is to research how the introduction of this species has caused changes to the existing interactions among native populations, and provide possible solutions for the problem.

The red lionfish is an invasive species that is causing much damage to the ecosystem in the Gulf of Mexico.

## Number of Lionfish Sightings

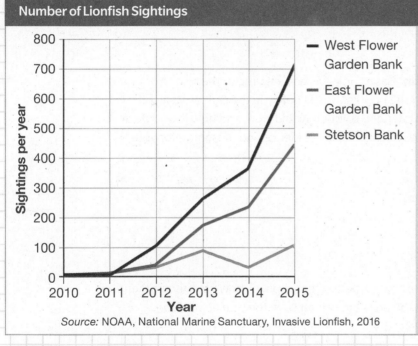

— West Flower Garden Bank

— East Flower Garden Bank

— Stetson Bank

*Source:* NOAA, National Marine Sanctuary, Invasive Lionfish, 2016

The number of lionfish sightings has greatly increased in recent years. This graph shows population sizes in three different areas in the Florida Garden Banks National Marine Sanctuary. In each area, the sightings of lionfish have been increasing.

**The steps below will help guide your research and develop your recommendation.**

### Engineer It

1. **Define the Problem**  Write a statement defining the problem you will be researching and recommending solutions for. Consider how this problem began and what impact it has on local ecosystems. What questions do you have about this problem?

**Engineer It**

2. **Conduct Research** Investigate lionfish and their impact on other species living in the Gulf of Mexico. How do lionfish interact with native species? How do they affect the availability of resources for native species? What is being done to try to control their population size?

3. **Construct an Explanation** Consider what you have learned about survival and interactions between living things. Explain why lionfish have been able to thrive as an invasive species in the Gulf of Mexico.

4. **Recommend a Solution** Based on your research, recommend one or more solutions for controlling the population of lionfish in the Gulf of Mexico. Explain how your recommended solution would work and how it would affect native species in the ecosystem. Provide evidence and reasoning for your recommendation.

5. **Communicate** Prepare a presentation that explains how your recommended solution would address the problem of lionfish in the Gulf of Mexico.

✓ **Self-Check**

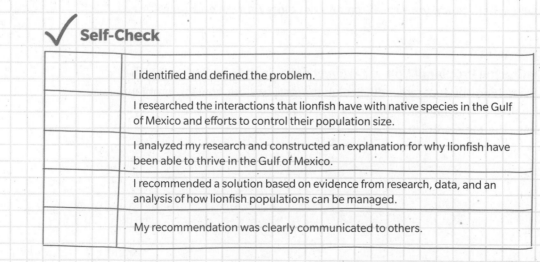

|  | I identified and defined the problem. |
|  | I researched the interactions that lionfish have with native species in the Gulf of Mexico and efforts to control their population size. |
|  | I analyzed my research and constructed an explanation for why lionfish have been able to thrive in the Gulf of Mexico. |
|  | I recommended a solution based on evidence from research, data, and an analysis of how lionfish populations can be managed. |
|  | My recommendation was clearly communicated to others. |

# Ecosystem Dynamics

The size and salt-level of the Great Salt Lake in Utah change over time. As water evaporates, salt deposits are left behind.

Humans use up to 40,000 different species for food, clothing, shelter, and medicines. The diversity of organisms, or *biodiversity*, is therefore very important to people. In addition to providing resources, diverse ecosystems are generally healthy ecosystems that provide valuable services such as water purification. What do you think would happen if there were an ecosystem change that resulted in a loss of biodiversity? In this unit, you will investigate ecosystem changes and the importance of maintaining biodiversity.

# Why It Matters

Here are some questions to consider as you work through the unit. Can you answer any of the questions now? Revisit these questions at the end of the unit to apply what you discover.

| Questions | Notes |
|---|---|
| What kinds of changes have you observed to natural areas in your community? | |
| What kinds of changes might people make to an ecosystem? | |
| How have ecosystems near you changed over the last 100 years? | |
| What types of organisms lived in your area 100 years ago? Do they all still live there? | |
| How could you determine if ecosystems near you are healthy? | |
| How can people help to maintain biodiversity in your community? | |
| What factors should be considered before introducing a new species to an area? | |

## Unit Starter: Predicting Effects of Ecosystem Change

Hawks are the top predator in this grasslands food web. Humans have cut down trees in many grassland ecosystems, which the hawks use for nesting. Think about the effects of a decreased hawk population in this food web.

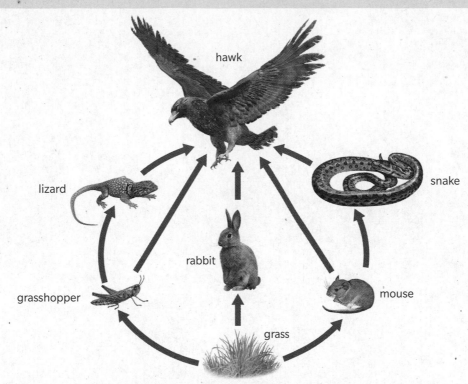

1. Predict what would happen if the hawk population decreased. Select all that apply.

   **A.** Rabbits would start eating grasshoppers and mice.

   **B.** The population of lizards, rabbits, and snakes would grow.

   **C.** The grass would become sparse because there would be more rabbits eating it.

   **D.** The grasshopper and mice populations would not be affected.

2. Imagine a similar ecosystem food web that includes an additional top predator — an owl population. These owls eat the same food as the hawks. In the ecosystem with owls, a decrease in the hawk population would have a *smaller/larger* impact on the rest of the ecosystem compared to the ecosystem without owls.

*Go online to download the Unit Project Worksheet to help you plan your project.*

## Unit Project

# Evaluate Biodiversity Design Solutions

Research an ecosystem scenario related to maintaining biodiversity. Analyze the design problem and potential solutions. Evaluate proposed solutions against criteria and constraints, including an explanation of how a chosen solution would affect populations and ecosystem services.

# Biodiversity in Ecosystems

This coral reef ecosystem in Thailand is home to a large number and variety of animals and other organisms.

**By the end of this lesson . . .**

you will be able to relate an ecosystem's biodiversity to its ability to recover from change.

**Go online** to view the digital version of the Hands-On Lab for this lesson and to download additional lab resources.

## CAN YOU EXPLAIN IT?

**What factors might have influenced how this ecosystem recovered from such a large and sudden flood?**

before flood

during flood

Several days of heavy rains caused the Vltava River in the Czech Republic to flood extensively in 2002. Towns and cities as well as the natural environment were all affected by this sudden disturbance. Some areas recovered more quickly than others.

1. Construct a cause-and-effect statement about the ecosystem shown in these two photos.

2. What types of living things do you think would be first to return or regrow after the floodwaters recede?

**EVIDENCE NOTEBOOK** As you explore this lesson, gather evidence to help explain what factors influence ecosystem recovery after a flood.

# Describing Biodiversity

Forests, salt marshes, deserts, and lakes are all examples of ecosystems. An ecosystem can be a small pond or extend across a vast grassland. Although there are many different types of ecosystems, they all have some common features. An **ecosystem** is a system made up of all the living and nonliving things in a given area. The living parts of an ecosystem interact with each other and with nonliving parts. Because of these interactions, ecosystems are dynamic—they are always changing. For example, the living components shown in the photos constantly interact with the nonliving and other living components. The macaques, a type of monkey, take in oxygen by breathing air and eat mostly plants and insects. The sea stars take in oxygen from the water through their feet and eat mostly mollusks.

This land ecosystem in Morocco contains several populations of organisms, including the endangered Barbary macaque. Macaques live alongside humans in certain parts of Morocco.

This marine ecosystem also contains several populations of organisms, including sea stars and mollusks. They live alongside many types of fish and coral in this ecosystem.

3. Fill in the table by listing the components in the word bank as living or nonliving parts of the ecosystems in the photos.

**WORD BANK**
- water
- plants
- sand
- air
- fish
- rocks
- macaques
- algae

| Living | Nonliving |
|---|---|
| | water |
| | |
| | |
| | |

# Biodiversity

One way to evaluate the health of an ecosystem is to consider its biodiversity.
**Biodiversity** refers to the variety of life in Earth's land, freshwater, and marine
ecosystems. Biodiversity can be studied at different scales. Scales can range from a
small area, such as a drop of water, to a large area, such as a forest. An area's biodiversity
may be made up of a few species or thousands of species. High biodiversity exists
when there are many species and individuals of those species living in an ecosystem.
Low biodiversity exists when there is a low number of species in an ecosystem. The
biodiversity of an area can be described as the combination of genetic diversity, species
diversity, and ecosystem diversity.

## Levels of Biodiversity

**Genetic diversity** refers to the variation
of genes within a species or population in a
given area. For example, the coyotes living
in this prairie may vary in body size, leg
length, fur color, or other characteristics.
These characteristics are passed, through
genes, from generation to generation.
All the possible genetic variations of
the coyotes in this prairie make up the
population's genetic diversity.

**Species diversity** refers to both the
number of different species that are in
a given area as well as the number of
individuals of each species that are there. In
this prairie, you can see a variety of plants
and animals. If you could see more of this
ecosystem, you would most likely see
more species. These species interact with
each other and with the nonliving parts of
the prairie ecosystem.

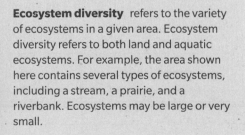

**Ecosystem diversity** refers to the variety
of ecosystems in a given area. Ecosystem
diversity refers to both land and aquatic
ecosystems. For example, the area shown
here contains several types of ecosystems,
including a stream, a prairie, and a
riverbank. Ecosystems may be large or very
small.

4. Which statement best describes an example of low species diversity?

   **A.** A population of chorus frogs has a wide variety of skin colors.

   **B.** A marsh ecosystem is covered by a single species of cattail bulrushes.

   **C.** A state park includes multiple forest, wetland, and freshwater ecosystems.

## Hands-On Lab
# Measure Biodiversity

Tricolor bumblebees nest on the ground in colonies.

Conduct a simulated measurement of two types of biodiversity of bumblebees in an area: species richness and species abundance.

Bumblebees are important pollinators of plants and crops. Humans rely on them to pollinate food crops. Suppose you are surveying bumblebees within a tall-grass prairie ecosystem. Your job is to provide an estimate of their biodiversity.

### MATERIALS
- jar of beans (containing 6 different types of dried beans)
- scoop of beans from jar
- scoop or cup, small

## Procedure and Analysis

**STEP 1** Observe the jar of beans. It is a model of the bumblebee population found in a tall-grass prairie ecosystem. The different bean types represent the different bumblebee species. Decide which bean type will represent each species and record this information in the table.

**STEP 2** Take a scoop of beans from the jar. These beans represent individual bumblebees from your sample area.

**STEP 3** *Species richness* refers to the number of different species found in a given area. What is the species richness of your sample area?

**STEP 4** *Species abundance* refers to the number of individuals of each species found in a given area. Record in the table the species abundance for each species found in your sample area.

**STEP 5** **Do the Math** Determine the relative species abundance for each species in the sample area. Relative species abundance will be reported as a percentage. Record your data in the table.

$$\text{Relative abundance} = \frac{\text{species abundance}}{\text{total number of bumblebees in sample}} \times 100$$

### Data for Sample Area

| Bumblebee species | Bean type | Species abundance | Relative abundance |
|---|---|---|---|
| Common eastern | | | |
| Rusty patched | | | |
| American | | | |
| Two-spotted | | | |
| Tricolored | | | |
| Brown-belted | | | |

**STEP 6** Draw a second table on a sheet of paper and combine your data with the data from the rest of the class. What is the species richness according to class data?

**STEP 7** Record species abundance in the class data table. Calculate and record relative species abundance using the overall class data.

**STEP 8** How did your data differ from the overall class data? What might account for any differences? Discuss these questions in small groups. Then share ideas and listen to others in a whole-class discussion.

**STEP 9** Develop hypotheses about the size of the scoop of beans you would need to be able to accurately measure different types of biodiversity and to sample rare bumblebee species in the ecosystem.

## Identify Patterns in Biodiversity

A variety of factors, including location, climate, and resource availability, can affect an ecosystem's biodiversity. Certain regions of Earth have very high biodiversity compared to other regions. Some of these regions have been identified as biodiversity hotspots. A *biodiversity hotspot* is a region that has high biodiversity and is threatened with possible destruction. Some land and marine hotspots are identified on the map.

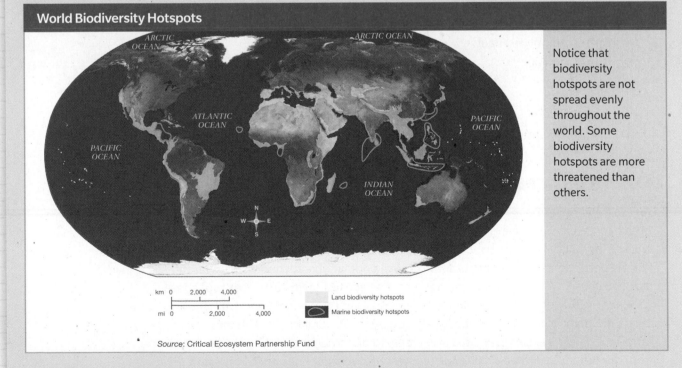

**World Biodiversity Hotspots**

Notice that biodiversity hotspots are not spread evenly throughout the world. Some biodiversity hotspots are more threatened than others.

km  0    2,000    4,000
mi  0         2,000    4,000

Land biodiversity hotspots
Marine biodiversity hotspots

*Source*: Critical Ecosystem Partnership Fund

5. Biodiversity hotspots are common near the equator / poles.
   Hotspots include ecosystems on land only / land and in water.

# Evaluating Ecosystem Health

Changes to an ecosystem can affect how the parts of an ecosystem interact. Within a healthy ecosystem, however, factors stay more or less within a certain range and in a mostly stable condition, even as individual parts change. Ecologists call this phenomenon *ecosystem stability*. Recall that matter and energy flow among the living and nonliving parts of an ecosystem. A change to any part of an ecosystem may disrupt the flow of energy and matter.

**Ecosystem Interactions Include the Flow of Energy and Matter**

Sunlight is the original source of energy in this desert ecosystem.

Plants use energy from sunlight to transform water and carbon dioxide into sugars and oxygen during photosynthesis. The plants take in water from the soil and carbon dioxide from the air. They use the sugars they make as food.

These burros eat plants in the Sonoran desert. Energy and matter move from the plants into the burros.

6. Suppose a new animal is introduced into this desert ecosystem. The animal has no natural predators. It eats the same plants the wild burros do. Which parts of the ecosystem might be affected by this change? Choose all that apply.

   A. other animals

   B. plants

   C. flow of energy

   D. cycling of matter

## Disturbances in Ecosystems

An *ecosystem disturbance* is a change in environmental conditions that causes a change in an ecosystem. Both living and nonliving parts of an ecosystem can be affected by a disturbance. Natural disturbances include wildfires, storms, flooding, tsunamis, and volcanic eruptions. Sudden increases in animal populations, such as insect swarms, can also cause a disturbance. Humans can create ecosystem disturbances too. These changes include oil spills, fires, and the clearing of land to harvest trees. Humans also clear land to make space for agriculture, housing, roads, or industry. The removal or introduction of a species in an area also creates a disturbance. Ecosystems can recover from disturbances. How quickly an ecosystem recovers depends on the type and severity of the disturbance.

## An Ecosystem Disturbance

A landslide greatly affected this ecosystem in the Philippines. The land was covered by mud and rocks that removed plants and displaced people and other animals.

This photo shows the same ecosystem just one year after the landslide. Plants are growing on the landslide mud. Animals and people have returned to live in the area.

The biodiversity of an ecosystem that experiences a disturbance can influence how well the ecosystem recovers. Ecosystems with high biodiversity have many species fulfilling certain roles, such as pollinator, decomposer, and predator. The graphic below shows how ecosystems with high and low biodiversity can be affected by disturbances.

## Biodiversity Impacts Ecosystem Stability

This graphic models the stability of four different ecosystems during years with different amounts of rainfall. The different-colored dots represent different species of insect pollinators. Some of these insects do better in high-rainfall years. Others do better in low-rainfall years.

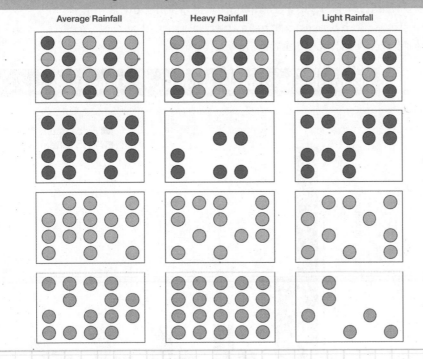

**Diverse community** Some species do better in wetter years. Others do better in drier years. The total number of pollinators remains stable.

**Community made up mostly of red species** This pollinator species is negatively affected by high rainfall.

**Community made up of mostly green species** This pollinator species survives dry and wet years equally well.

**Community made up of mostly blue species** This pollinator species is negatively affected by low rainfall.

7. In your own words, explain how rainfall could influence the species abundance over time in the different communities. In which ecosystem is the least amount of change observed in the abundance of pollinators?

# Biodiversity and Ecosystem Health

The health of an ecosystem includes its ability to recover from a disturbance. Ecological diversity, species diversity, and genetic diversity all contribute to ecosystem stability. A diverse ecosystem has more ways to recover from a disturbance. If one species dies or leaves a diverse ecosystem, another species can take its place. As a result, the ecosystem can stabilize more quickly.

An ecosystem with lowered biodiversity is less able to recover from a disturbance. Some ecosystems, such as those in polar regions, can maintain stability while naturally having lower biodiversity than warmer regions. Ecosystems generally become less stable when their biodiversity levels are lowered from their baseline levels.

 **EVIDENCE NOTEBOOK**

8. How would biodiversity levels affect the recovery of ecosystems along the Vltava River after the floodwaters recede? Record your evidence.

 **Do the Math**

# Assess Ecosystem Health

Having many different species in an ecosystem is a sign of high-species diversity. But the size of each population of species is also important. A population can be too small. Fewer individuals means there is less genetic diversity in a population. The graph shows the biodiversity of birds in two ecosystems. Both ecosystems have an equal amount of species diversity. However, they are different in some significant ways.

9. What are the main differences in species abundance between the populations of birds in the two ecosystems?

10. Given the data in the graph, what can you predict about how each ecosystem might recover from a disturbance?

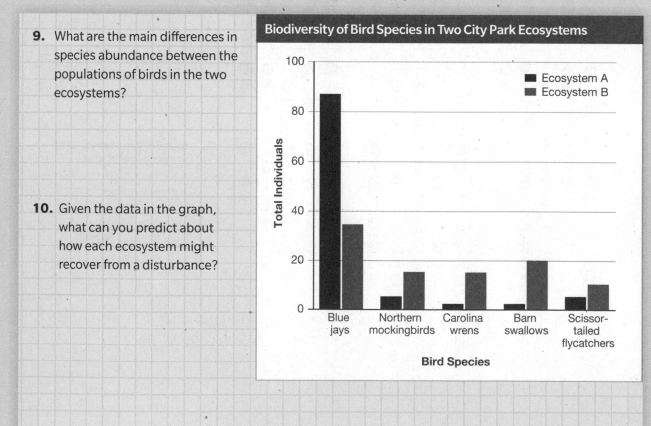

Biodiversity of Bird Species in Two City Park Ecosystems

# Analyzing Human Influences on Biodiversity

Humans have designed structures and developed processes that help them survive in their environments. Ecosystems provide the energy and raw materials that humans need to live and survive. For example, we use wood from trees to build homes. We burn wood and fossil fuels to provide energy. Humans rely on ecosystems to grow crops and raise livestock. Humans also depend on the nonliving parts of ecosystems for clean air, fresh water, and living space. In this way, humans can also affect the health and biodiversity of ecosystems.

Explore ONLINE!

Humans introduced the European honeybee (*Apis mellifera*) to the United States. These bees make honey and beeswax.

**11.** Humans rely on certain services that ecosystems provide. Which ecosystem processes below do humans benefit from? Circle all that apply.

**A.** decomposition of wastes

**B.** pollination of crops

**C.** filtering of fresh water

**D.** growth of trees and plants

## Humans Are Part of Earth's Ecosystems

We depend on healthy ecosystems for survival and for a good quality of life. For example, every time you breathe or drink a glass of water, you depend on ecosystem processes to provide oxygen and fresh, clean water. Healthy ecosystems buffer the impact of storms, limit the spread of disease, and recycle nutrients. Humans rely on ecosystems to reduce the effects of droughts and floods, provide fertile soils, pollinate crops and plants, disperse seeds, and control pests by natural predators. For these reasons and more, high biodiversity in ecosystems is important to all humans. Humans benefit from ecosystems with high biodiversity because ecosystem health and ecosystem services are related to biodiversity.

# Negative Impacts on Biodiversity

Human activities affect the biodiversity of ecosystems. Although we rely on healthy ecosystems, many human activities negatively affect biodiversity. Some activities cause direct negative effects, such as overharvesting of plants or animals. Other activities cause indirect negative effects. For example, constructing new buildings can destroy habitats and reduce biodiversity. Releasing garbage and pollution into the environment can harm or poison organisms and reduce biodiversity.

## Habitat Destruction

Activities such as the construction of roads, buildings, towns, and cities cause habitat destruction. Mining and harvesting resources also remove habitats. Less habitat means less biodiversity on all scales—ecosystem, species, and genetic. Human activity can also break large habitats into smaller pieces. When a habitat is broken into smaller pieces, animals that need a large area of habitat can no longer live there.

Habitat destruction occurs when land is cleared for development.

## Introduced Species

Tulips, orange trees, and many other highly valued plants are now grown in the United States. However, they are not native to the country. People introduced them to a new environment when they brought them from other countries. These non-native species are called *introduced species*. Introduced species can have negative impacts on ecosystems. For example, buckthorn, lionfish, emerald ash borers, and Burmese pythons are invasive organisms that threaten native species in several United States ecosystems. These species do not have predators or other natural factors in their new environments that limit their populations' growth.

Pet Burmese pythons that were released into the wild threaten biodiversity in areas of South Florida.

## Overharvested Species

Many fish species are harvested for food. The overharvesting of certain fish species threatens marine biodiversity. For example, decades of overfishing led to an extreme drop in populations of Atlantic cod in the early 1990s. This almost caused the collapse of the cod fishing industry. The fishing of Atlantic cod in the north Atlantic was banned in 1992. Overharvesting of plants such as coneflowers and American ginseng has greatly reduced their wild population sizes. Land animal species such as tigers have also been hunted, sometimes to extinction. When a population is reduced to a very small size due to overharvesting, genetic diversity is lost.

Atlantic cod populations are closely monitored and are slowly recovering from near extinction in the early 1990s.

## Lack of Biodiversity in Food Crops

Many of today's food crops have very little genetic diversity. Some crops, such as bananas, are all genetically identical. Recall that genetic diversity in a population increases the likelihood that some members of a population will survive a disturbance such as a disease. Genetically identical food crops are more likely to be destroyed by a disturbance because every plant reacts in the same way. In the case of bananas, a fungal disease, called *Panama disease,* is destroying banana plants. This disease is threatening banana crops and the livelihood of the people who grow and sell them.

Scientists are working on reintroducing into crops some of the wild-type genes that were lost during domestication. The intention of this bioengineering is to make hardier crops. The wild cousins of crop plants tend to be better able to survive disturbances. Scientists hope that reintroducing wild genes into crop plants will create crops that are more pest and drought resistant and better able to take in nutrients from the soil.

**EVIDENCE NOTEBOOK**

**12.** Look at the image of the ecosystem before the flood. How have humans changed the area and how might this affect recovery after the flood? Record your evidence.

## Efforts to Protect Biodiversity

Not all human activities negatively affect biodiversity. Around the globe, people are working to limit the negative impact of human activity and preserve biodiversity. In many locations, nature preserves have been created to protect habitats. Wildlife corridors have been created to connect areas of natural habitat divided by roads or development. Awareness of overharvesting has also become more common. This awareness promotes policies to prevent additional overharvesting and guide the recovery of populations. One way plant biodiversity has been supported is by creating seed banks around the world. These banks help preserve biodiversity by storing different types of plant seeds. Seed banks are a resource for plant breeders.

This forest is managed in a way that provides a sustainable source of wood for industry.

**13. Language SmArts** Write an argument about why people should work toward having positive influences on biodiversity. Support your claims with clear reasons and relevant evidence. Present your argument to the class.

## Engineer It

# Monitor and Preserve Biodiversity

Disrupting any part of an ecosystem can change its biodiversity. Suppose a builder clears a field to build houses. In the field, several wildflower species grow. Different animal species living in and around the field depended on the wildflowers for food. Without the food source, those species would die or move away.

Measuring biodiversity before and after a disturbance is one way to monitor changes in an ecosystem. For example, biodiversity counts can be taken before the field is cleared and again after the houses are built. Comparing these counts helps determine the effects the disturbance had on the health of the area. Solutions can be incorporated into building designs to help preserve and protect biodiversity that may be affected by a development.

**14.** How might biodiversity count data be used to design a solution for maintaining biodiversity at a new housing development?

_____

_____

_____

_____

_____

_____

_____

_____

A grid is a tool used to mark sample areas and survey biodiversity. The species within the grid are counted.

**15.** Describe a design problem that is addressed by the rooftop garden on the building shown in the photo.

_____

_____

_____

_____

_____

_____

The plants on this rooftop are part of a solution to minimize the impact that concrete, asphalt, roof tiles, and other non-absorbent surfaces have on the surrounding environment.

**16.** Write either a + or a − sign to identify a positive or negative impact on biodiversity.

_____ planting native plants that support native pollinators

_____ collecting rainwater to reuse for irrigation

_____ building a "rain garden" to promote filtering of runoff after rainfall

_____ constructing a road that divides habitat that was once connected

_____ clearing of land to build new buildings

# Continue Your Exploration

Name: _____  Date: _____

**Check out the path below or go online to choose one of the other paths shown.**

Careers in Science

- **Hands-On Lab** 👋
- **You Are an Ecosystem**
- **Propose Your Own Path**

Go online to choose one of these other paths.

## Restoration Ecologist

Restoration ecology is a field that focuses on restoring freshwater, marine, and land ecosystems that have been damaged by human activity. Restoration ecologists help design solutions to problems facing ecosystems. These solutions help preserve biodiversity. Restoration ecologists may provide assistance to government agencies and to businesses.

Some jobs restoration ecologists might do include:

- controlling and removing invasive species
- helping farmers to use sustainable farming practices
- working to improve habitats for specific species
- planning and developing practices for soil or land conservation
- planning and implementing the restoration of ocean, lake, or stream shorelines

Restoration ecologists may work alone or with others, in the field or in an office. They often collect data in the field and return to an office or laboratory to analyze the data. Then they develop a solution to the biodiversity problem. They may use mapping and computer modeling to help in developing these solutions. Other science disciplines use similar methods and equipment to obtain and evaluate evidence. Accurately collecting and analyzing evidence and applying conclusions in a valid manner is the nature of science.

This restoration ecologist is collecting data to study the change in plant communities at a nature reserve in southern England.

143

# Continue Your Exploration

This landfill in New York was in operation for many decades.

Through restoration and engineering efforts, the landfill is being transformed into a park that includes wildlife habitats.

1. An organization wants to restore an area's ecosystem to attract bird species that used to live there. How might a restoration ecologist help them?

2. Look at the photos of the landfill area and its restoration. Describe at least two ways that changes to living and nonliving components of the ecosystem have positively affected the biodiversity of the area.

3. What types of evidence might help determine whether the restored ecosystem has high biodiversity?

4. **Collaborate** With a group, outline a restoration project in an area in your community. Suppose that you and your classmates are the restoration ecologists planning and carrying out the work. Develop a short presentation of your proposal. Include an explanation for how the project would positively affect biodiversity in the area.

# Can You Explain It?

Name: _____     Date: _____

What factors might have influenced how this ecosystem recovered from such a large and sudden flood?

before flood

during flood

**EVIDENCE NOTEBOOK**

Refer to the notes in your Evidence Notebook to help you construct an explanation for how this ecosystem might have recovered from such a huge and sudden disturbance.

1. State your claim. Make sure your claim fully explains how this ecosystem might have recovered from the flood.

2. Summarize the evidence you have gathered to support your claim and explain your reasoning.

# Checkpoints

**Answer the following questions to check your understanding of the lesson.**

**Use the photo to answer Question 3.**

3. What can you tell about this population of king penguins and their icy Sandwich Island ecosystem from the photo? Choose all that apply.

   A. There is low genetic diversity in this population of king penguins.

   B. It is likely to be one of the largest bird populations in the ecosystem.

   C. Not a lot of species diversity can be seen in this photo.

   D. A lot of species diversity is shown in this photo.

4. An ecosystem with high / low biodiversity is better able to recover from a disturbance because the more biodiverse an ecosystem is, the more / less likely it is that some organisms will survive and continue to grow.

**Use the photo to answer Question 5.**

5. This photo shows restoration efforts at a former open-pit mine. How will the restoration of this land most likely affect populations of organisms in the surrounding area?

   A. Biodiversity will likely increase.

   B. Population sizes will likely decrease.

   C. Stability will likely decrease.

   D. Disturbances will likely increase.

6. In order to make crop growing more economical, crops such as wheat, corn, and potatoes are often grown on large areas of land where all other plants have been removed. Why can this type of planting style make crops more prone to outbreaks of disease?

   A. The high species diversity associated with croplands leads to poor crop health.

   B. Biodiversity of the cultivated land where the crops grow is very low.

   C. Genetic diversity in crops is typically high, leading to more disease outbreaks.

   D. All ecosystems managed by humans have low biodiversity and poor health.

# Interactive Review

**Complete this section to review the main concepts of the lesson.**

Biodiversity refers to the variety of life that is a part of Earth's ecosystems. Biodiversity can be studied at the ecosystem, species, and genetic level.

**A.** Explain why it is important to consider all three levels of biodiversity rather than just one.

An *ecosystem disturbance* is a temporary change in environmental conditions that causes a change in an ecosystem. The health of an ecosystem can be defined by its ability to recover or remain stable when a disturbance occurs.

**B.** What evidence is used as an indicator of ecosystem health? Explain your answer.

Humans, just like other organisms, need healthy ecosystems in which to survive, but many human activities have negative effects on ecosystems and their biodiversity.

**C.** Describe how humans can influence biodiversity by using specific examples.

# Changes in Ecosystems

Bare rock is exposed for the first time in thousands of years after a glacier retreats from Aialik Bay in Kenai Fjords National Park, Alaska.

**By the end of this lesson . . .**

you will be able to explain how changes in an ecosystem can affect populations within it.

© Houghton Mifflin Harcourt • Image Credits: ©Phil Schermeister/National Geographic/Getty Images

## CAN YOU EXPLAIN IT?

### How can a swarm of millions of desert locusts affect an ecosystem?

Desert locusts look and act a lot like grasshoppers, although they are larger. They normally eat plants and live alone. However, certain changes in environmental conditions, such as a drought, can cause them to come together in swarms to travel long distances to find food.

1. Why might a drought cause normally solitary desert locusts to change their behavior and swarm?

2. How might swarming locusts affect planted crops? How might the swarms affect local populations of humans and insect-eating birds?

 **EVIDENCE NOTEBOOK** As you explore the lesson, gather evidence to help explain how an insect swarm can affect an ecosystem.

# Describing Changes in Ecosystems

Yikes! You lift up a rotting log from a forest floor and several insects dash away from it. You disturbed their ecosystem! An *ecosystem* is a natural system in which organisms interact with the living and nonliving parts of their environment.

Insects are not the only living things in a forest floor ecosystem. You might also observe spiders, fungi, snails, mosses, worms, or a toad. Vines, ferns, and other plants might also grow on the forest floor. All of these living organisms depend on each other and the nonliving parts of the ecosystem. The nonliving parts include rocks, nutrients, air, and water. The log lying on the forest floor is no longer alive. Yet, it supports lots of life. Some living things break down the log's cells for food. This decomposition releases nutrients from the log back into the soil. In this way, energy and matter cycle between the living and nonliving parts of an ecosystem.

▷ *Explore* ONLINE!

### Forest Floor Ecosystem

Ecosystems, even tiny ones, contain living and nonliving parts that interact. Plants take in minerals from the soil and carbon dioxide from the air. Snails eat plants. They also eat soil to get calcium for their shells.

3. A system input is any energy, matter, or information that enters a system. Which factors would be inputs of a forest floor ecosystem? Select the correct answers.

   A. soil

   B. sunlight

   C. rain

   D. trees

4. **Discuss** How do you think a decrease in one of these inputs would affect the forest floor ecosystem?

# Ecosystems Change Over Time

Ecosystems are also dynamic, which means their characteristics can change over time. Even healthy ecosystems with high biodiversity change a bit every day. In every ecosystem, organisms are born, some die, and all living things respond to changes. Ecosystems with high biodiversity can recover from changes more easily than those with less diversity. Some changes, such as the seasons, are gradual. Other changes, such as a storm or a flood, are sudden.

**Seasonal Changes**

spring • summer • fall • winter

Changes in temperature, precipitation and sunlight occur during the seasons. They cause changes in ecosystems. This tree goes from budding new leaves in spring to full bloom in summer. Then it loses its leaves in the fall and is inactive through the winter.

**5.** Classify each statement as a change to a living factor or a change to a nonliving factor.

| Change | Change to Living Factor | Change to Nonliving Factor |
|---|---|---|
| Birds migrate in fall. | | |
| Ice that covers lakes melts in spring. | | |
| Temperature increases in summer. | | |
| Leaves fall from trees in fall. | | |
| Seeds sprout in spring. | | |
| Water in soil freezes in winter. | | |

**6.** Some bird populations that live in the northern hemisphere migrate to warmer climates for the winter. Identify likely reasons birds would respond this way to a seasonal change in their habitat.

## Gradual Changes

Gradual changes to ecosystems are going on all the time in every ecosystem. For example, changes may take place slowly in a pond or lake. Sediment builds up over time in a body of water. It eventually changes the area into level land. Sediment buildup also leads to natural *eutrophication*. During this process, nutrients from plants and rock minerals dissolve in the pond water. They help plants and algae grow. When the plants and algae die, they fall to the bottom of the pond.

Over time dead plant and algal material builds up. Organisms living in the pond ecosystem will change in response to the change. Fish, amphibians, and insects that live in water would eventually move away to find another pond, or predators may eat them. Eventually, all populations living in the pond ecosystem will be affected by the change. Gradual changes also take place as glaciers melt, logs rot, and climates change. Even a relatively small increase in temperatures can have a widespread effect on ecosystems.

Over a long period of time, this pond filled up with sediment and changed into a meadow.

sediment builds up

7. The effects of the change to the pond will most likely be short-term / long-term as the pond ecosystem changes to a meadow. The living and nonliving parts of the ecosystems will change / stay the same.

## Sudden Changes

Forest fires, tornadoes, volcanic eruptions, and floods can all cause a sudden change to an ecosystem. For example, if a river floods, it may burst its banks. Its banks may erode and cause the river water to become too muddy or too fast flowing for fish and other river organisms to survive. Living things that depended on fish for food may be negatively affected because their food source is gone.

Sudden changes happen quickly and can kill or remove several populations of organisms from an ecosystem at once. Similarly to a slow change, sudden changes can be local or widespread. An event that causes changes to the living or nonliving parts of an ecosystem is called a **disturbance**. Some disturbances are natural processes. Other disturbances are caused by humans when they damage or remove parts of an ecosystem.

In just minutes, a tornado causes a sudden ecosystem change. Powerful winds rip trees and other plants from the soil and may kill or displace many animals.

**8.** The photos show two different ecosystems after sudden changes. Compare and contrast these two changes. Write your answer in the space provided.

This forest fire caused several changes in the forest habitat. A wildfire can travel about three meters per second.

Ash, gases, and lava flow from a volcanic eruption affect the area around the volcano. Lava can flow about eight meters per second.

**9.** How do you think these two sudden changes might affect the living and nonliving parts of the ecosystems?

## Effects of Changes in Ecosystems

Since each part of an ecosystem is interconnected, a change to any part can affect the larger ecosystem. Consider a population in an ecosystem that is removed for some reason. Another species or population in the same ecosystem may fill the "gap" left by the missing species. Or the species might not be replaced at all.

For example, suppose a disease killed one species of bee in an ecosystem. Bees are important pollinators in many ecosystems. Another bee species living in the same area might now have more food and living space. It could become the main pollinator in the area. But, if the diseased bee species were the only bee species in the area, there may not be another species to fill the ecological "role" as pollinators. Flowers and other plants would not be pollinated by bees. This would mean fewer insect-pollinated plants would grow in the future. There would also be less food such as seeds, fruit, and vegetables for animals that depend on insect-pollinated plants.

**EVIDENCE NOTEBOOK**

**10.** Think about the swarm of locusts you saw at the beginning of the lesson. Is the swarm a change to a living or a nonliving ecosystem component? Is the change gradual or sudden? Record your evidence.

# Recovering from Disturbances

After a disturbance, an ecosystem begins to recover. **Succession** is the process of recovery and change that happens after a disturbance. Sometimes the original community may grow back. Other times the changes to an ecosystem are so severe that populations that once lived there die out or do not return. Then, succession begins when certain organisms, called *pioneer species*, begin to grow. For example, after a glacier retreats, only bare rock remains. Pioneer species such as lichens can grow on rock and help to form soil. Over time, soil forms and other plants and animals return. The ecosystem becomes more complex when it is able to support more types of organisms. Biodiversity gradually increases. The variety of species and number of individuals in a population tend to increase with time after a disturbance.

### Language SmArts
# Analyze Rate of Environmental Change

Artificial eutrophication results from pollution caused by humans. It happens when runoff from farm fertilizers, mining, or household waste adds large amounts of nutrients to a body of water. The large amount of nutrients supports algal blooms—population explosions of algae—in the water. As excess algae die, oxygen from the water is used as the algae decompose. The algae may also produce toxins that kill other living things, such as fish and amphibians. More oxygen is used up as their bodies decay. As a result, other organisms may not be able to live in the water.

Excess nutrients from fertilizer runoff caused a toxic bloom of cyanobacteria in the Copco Reservoir in California.

11. Excess nutrients in an aquatic ecosystem is a form of pollution. The pollution is an input / output of the lake ecosystem. Populations of birds in the area that feed on fish from the lake would likely stay / move away. As a result of eutrophication, the biodiversity of the lake ecosystem would likely increase / decrease.

12. If artificial eutrophication continues, what do you think will eventually happen to this ecosystem? Use evidence to explain your reasoning.

_____

_____

_____

_____

_____

_____

# Predicting Changes to Populations

An ecosystem disturbance can be caused by the introduction of a nonnative species, such as the introduction of eastern gray squirrels to Europe. Gray squirrels are native to the eastern United States. They were introduced to several locations in the United Kingdom and Ireland between 1876 and 1929. The species quickly adapted to their new forest ecosystems. The total population of gray squirrels in Europe has increased greatly since their introduction.

Red squirrels are native to Europe and northern Asia. Gray squirrels are larger and more aggressive than red squirrels. They eat a larger variety of foods. They also have fewer predators than red squirrels do. As a result, gray squirrels took over much of the red squirrels' resources and the red squirrel population decreased across Europe.

The eastern gray squirrel has quite a varied diet. It eats nuts, flowers, fruits, seeds, tree bark, fungi, frogs, eggs, and bird hatchlings.

Eurasian red squirrels prefer to eat the seeds of trees but will also eat berries, young plant shoots, and bird eggs.

**13.** Compare and contrast potential effects of two disturbances on a native population of red squirrels—a storm and the introduction of nonnative gray squirrels. Fill in the Venn diagram using the statements.

**WORD BANK**
- competes for resources
- decreases available food
- reduces available living space
- causes sudden change
- introduces disease

Gray squirrels

Both

Storm

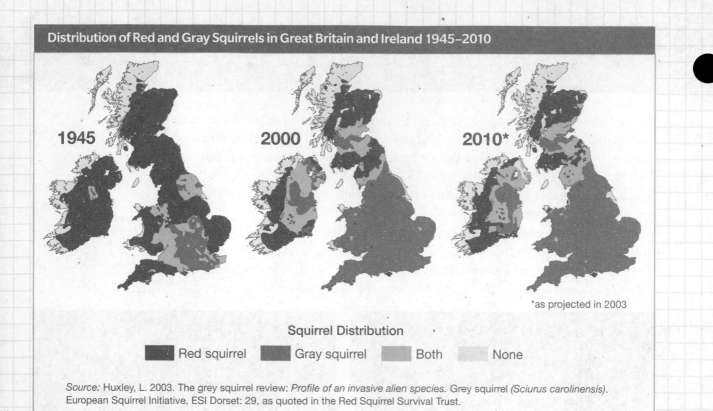

**Distribution of Red and Gray Squirrels in Great Britain and Ireland 1945–2010**

1945    2000    2010*

*as projected in 2003

**Squirrel Distribution**

Red squirrel     Gray squirrel     Both     None

*Source:* Huxley, L. 2003. The grey squirrel review: *Profile of an invasive alien species.* Grey squirrel *(Sciurus carolinensis)*. European Squirrel Initiative, ESI Dorset: 29, as quoted in the Red Squirrel Survival Trust.

**14. Language SmArts**  In your own words, describe the changes in the distribution of red and gray squirrels from 1945 to 2010.

The introduction of gray squirrels into Europe had a negative impact on populations of red squirrels. Scientists also identified that gray squirrels negatively affected populations of songbirds and likely spread the disease squirrelpox to red squirrels. Gray squirrels also eat the bark from trees in winter, causing the trees to be more prone to disease. However, the presence of gray squirrels helped another species to rebound from the point of extinction.

Scientists determined that gray squirrels likely had a positive effect on the populations of pine martens. Pine martens are weasel-like predators of squirrels. Pine martens were hunted to near extinction in the United Kingdom and Ireland in the early 20th century. Farmers and landowners considered them pests because they ate chickens and young lambs. Since pine martens became a protected species in the 1980s, their numbers have grown. Researchers noted that pine martens prefer eating gray squirrels to red squirrels. Gray squirrels are larger, slower, and spend more time on the ground. So pine martens can catch gray squirrels more easily. With more food, pine marten populations in Ireland and Scotland have increased, and the rate of gray squirrel population growth has decreased.

# Effects of Ecosystem Changes on Populations

Ecosystem components are connected, so changes to living or nonliving parts can affect populations. The removal of a single species, a reduced food source, or a change in temperature can cause large changes in the other parts of the ecosystems. For example, several years of increased average winter temperatures can cause seeds to germinate earlier and change the behavior of migrating animals.

A change may displace or kill individuals and populations. A large portion of a population may move because of a disturbance such as a flood and not return. If this happens, there may not be enough individuals to sustain the population in that area over time and the local population could die out.

Bangladesh, a country in South Asia, is prone to flooding because it is low-lying and has a long coastline. The frequent flooding affects human, animal, and plant populations.

**Do the Math**

# Identify Factors That Change Populations

Before the arrival of European settlers in the United States, about 46% of the land was forested. Early settlers spoke of towering white pine trees. White pines were one of the many native species that were heavily harvested for building ship masts, wagons, fences, and furniture. Clearing of old-growth forests for agriculture and commercial purposes hit its highest rate in the mid-1800s and continued until the mid-1920s.

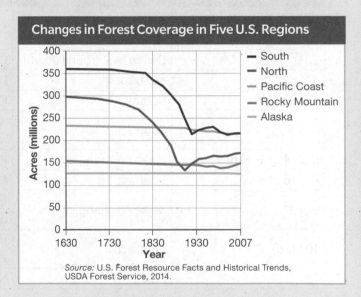

Changes in Forest Coverage in Five U.S. Regions

— South
— North
— Pacific Coast
— Rocky Mountain
— Alaska

*Source:* U.S. Forest Resource Facts and Historical Trends, USDA Forest Service, 2014.

15. What information about forest coverage does the graph tell you?

16. The Carolina parakeet once lived in large flocks in old-growth forests in the eastern and southeastern United States. Their extinction has been linked to the removal of old-growth forests. Based on the graph, when do you think Carolina parakeet populations decreased the most? Give a reason for your answer.

## Hands-On Lab
# What Factors Influence a Population Change?

You will simulate population changes in a pack of wolves. Then you will identify specific changes that affect the population of wolves.

**MATERIALS**
- cup
- dice (2)
- pencil
- popcorn kernels (generous handful)

## Procedure

**STEP 1** Place eight popcorn kernels on the table. Two kernels represent adult wolves, the other six represent a litter of pups.

**STEP 2** Follow the game play key that is shown below. The game play key will allow you to model ecosystem changes that affect a wolf population by throwing the dice. Some of the changes to the ecosystem are natural events and some are caused by humans.

| If you roll . . . | You . . . | Reason |
|---|---|---|
| Double 2s, 3s, 4s, 5s, or 6s | Subtract 3 | Nursing female ingests rat poison; pups die |
| 2 | Divide by 2 (round down) | Disease introduced by stray dogs; half the pack dies |
| 3 | Subtract 4 | Drought occurs, causing food shortage for prey |
| 4 (1+3) | Subtract 1 | One wolf dies of natural causes |
| 5 | Subtract 2 | A harmful pollutant builds up in the tissues of rabbits; wolves eat the rabbits and get poisoned |
| 6 (2+4 or 1+5) or 7 | Make no changes | Rains arrive; pack lives well for six months |
| 8 (2+6 or 3+5) | Subtract 1 | One pup dies of natural causes |
| 9 or 11 | Make no changes | Elk population remains high due to plentiful plant growth; wolves live well for six months |
| 10 (4+6) | Subtract 1 | Habitat size decreases due to development; male killed in territorial dispute with another wolf pack |
| 12 | Add 1 | New, mature wolf joins pack |

**STEP 3** On a separate sheet of paper make a table similar to the sample table below. The table should record the results of 15 years of data.

| Year | Last year's total | Add a litter (+6) | First 6 months | | Second 6 months | | Pack subtotal | Subtract matured pups? | Total pack for year |
|---|---|---|---|---|---|---|---|---|---|
| | | | Reason | Effect on pack | Reason | Effect on pack | | | |
| 1 | 2 | +6 | | | | | | no | |
| 2 | | | | | | | | no | |
| 3 | | | | | | | | | |

© Houghton Mifflin Harcourt

**STEP 4** Roll the dice to represent the passage of six months. Use the total number on the dice to determine what happens to your pack, according to the game play key. Then fill in the information in your data table. As you record data, also record in the *Reason* column the reason for the population change. Adjust the number of kernels that represent your wolf pack.

**STEP 5** Repeat Step 4 for the second six months of the year. Count the number of wolves in your pack and fill in the rest of Year 1 in the data table.

**STEP 6** Reproduction: After Year 1, adjust the number of kernels to add six pups at the beginning of each year unless a food shortage occurred the previous year.

**STEP 7** Maturation: When the pack gets too large, the mature pups leave. Subtract six wolves if your pack has more than nine wolves. Adjust the number of kernels you have accordingly. Record the pack total in the last column of the table.

**STEP 8** Repeat Steps 4–7 until you complete 15 years of play or until your pack dies out, whichever comes first.

## Analysis

**STEP 9** What patterns did you notice in the types of ecosystem changes that affected your wolf pack? Did a relatively small change have a larger impact on the wolf population? Explain your answer.

**STEP 10** How might a change to a wolf pack affect other populations, such as the elk or bison that the wolves feed on?

**STEP 11** Does evidence from your model suggest that many different types of changes correlate with changes in the wolf population? Explain your answer.

**EVIDENCE NOTEBOOK**

**17.** Desert locusts are plant eaters and are eaten by animals such as snakes, birds, and small mammals. What effects might the swarm of locusts have on other populations in an ecosystem? Record your evidence.

# Populations That Depend on Disturbance

In the early 1900s, a major goal of the United States Forestry Service was to stop forest fires. One reason for this effort was to prevent the destruction of timber resources. However, around the 1960s, scientists began to recognize that the fires are important to the health of forest ecosystems. They realized that a forest ecosystem becomes unhealthy if fires do not occur periodically. Scientists observed that if every fire is prevented, trees become overcrowded and dead plant material builds up on the forest floor. Today, scientists know that fires add nutrients to soil. Fires clear the forest floor, providing space for seedlings. They can also thin out the tree canopy, which allows more sunlight to reach the forest floor. Saplings and other plants can then grow.

Sequoias are adapted to survive forest fires. The trees depend on fires to reduce competition from other trees that may crowd out their germinating seedlings.

Some populations depend on fires. For example, populations of sequoias, a type of redwood tree, depend on forest fires to reproduce. They need low-intensity fires to release seeds from their cones. Forest fires also reduce competition from other species.

**Engineer It**

# Forest Fire Control Policy

Fire suppression is the process of preventing or putting out forest fires. It was a tool commonly used in the past to prevent forest fires. In the late 1890s, conservationists identified forest fires as a major threat to the U.S. economy because they destroyed the supply of timber. In 1910, the U.S. government began a policy of total fire suppression. The policy involved preventing fires and also putting out a fire as quickly as possible once one started. Later, researchers observed that the fire suppression policy had unintended effects on forest ecosystems. Populations of plants that depended on fires to complete their life cycles were negatively affected and forest ecosystems were changing. Such observations led to a policy change in the 1970s. Today, the U.S. National Park Service manages and controls, rather than totally extinguishes, forest fires.

**18.** Imagine you are a forest ranger. Define the engineering design problem you face in developing a solution to allow the fire-dependent plants in the forest you manage to carry out their life cycle. You want to minimize fire hazards for people who visit and live near the forest. You also need to be mindful of air pollution laws. List at least three criteria and constraints that would influence your solution.

_____

_____

_____

_____

# Continue Your Exploration

Name: _____          Date: _____

**Check out the path below or go online to choose one of the other paths shown.**

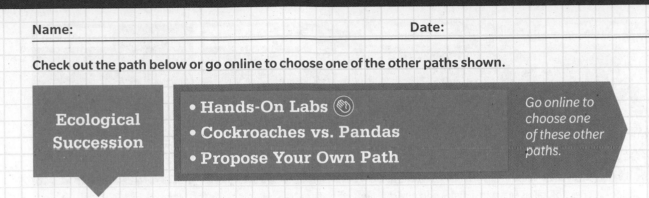

**Ecological Succession**

- **Hands-On Labs** ✋
- **Cockroaches vs. Pandas**
- **Propose Your Own Path**

*Go online to choose one of these other paths.*

Ecological succession is the process of regrowth and recovery in an ecosystem after a disturbance. The two main types of succession are distinguished by whether or not there is soil left after the disturbance.

In both types of succession, the number and variety of plants will increase over time as will the number and variety of animals.

## Primary Succession

Primary succession happens in an environment where a disturbance removed soil or exposed bare rock. It also describes the growth of vegetation in areas that previously did not have any plant growth. Lava flows, sand dune formations, and the retreat of glaciers create landscapes that go through primary succession. The earliest stage of primary succession involves the growth of lichens and mosses. The remains of dead mosses, lichens, and other organisms build up, forming soil. As soil builds up, grasses and other small plants begin to grow, followed by bushes and small trees. Eventually, there will be enough soil for trees to grow.

bare rock | lichens grow | mosses grow | grasses grow

Primary succession occurs after glaciers retreat. It may take hundreds or thousands of years for a mature ecosystem to develop.

## Secondary Succession

Secondary succession takes place after a disturbance disrupts ecosystem processes and removes some of the living parts of the ecosystem. Forest fires, flooding, and logging of trees by humans can lead to secondary succession. Because soil remains after the event, secondary succession takes place faster than primary succession. New and surviving plants grow relatively rapidly. At first, the plants that grow are small, but bushes and trees eventually grow.

# Continue Your Exploration

soil left intact  plant regrowth  small trees  mature forest

Secondary succession takes place in a disturbed environment when the soil is left intact. As the plant populations change in ecological succession, so too do the populations of fungi, protists, bacteria, and animals that live in the area.

1. The stages of ecological succession can be predicted by scientists. How is this possible?

2. Changes in the plant species in an area cause changes to populations of animal species in the area too. Propose a reason why this occurs.

3. Flash flood waters deposit a large amount of sediment called a *delta* at the mouth of a river. Plants grow on the delta and animals arrive soon after. Do you think this example is more similar to primary or secondary succession? Give reasons for your answer.

4. **Collaborate**  A volcano erupts on the sea floor, building an island of lava rock. Fifty years later, small areas of the island have a variety of plants. Birds nest on the island. Insects feed on plant parts. Working with a partner, construct a flow chart that uses evidence to explain primary succession on this volcanic island.

# Can You Explain It?

**Name:** _____     **Date:** _____

How can a swarm of millions of desert locusts affect an ecosystem?

 **EVIDENCE NOTEBOOK**

Refer to the notes in your Evidence Notebook to help you construct an explanation for how a swarm of locusts can affect an ecosystem.

1. State your claim. Make sure your claim fully explains how this disturbance could affect the ecosystem.

2. Summarize the evidence you have gathered to support your claim and explain your reasoning.

# Checkpoints

**Answer the following questions to check your understanding of the lesson.**

**Use the photo to answer Questions 3 and 4.**

3. A lahar is a mudflow made up of lava, water, and rocks. How might a lahar affect an ecosystem?

   a lahar

   **A.** It is a sudden disturbance that affects few populations in the affected area.

   **B.** It is a sudden disruption that affects all local populations in the affected area.

   **C.** It is a gradual disruption that affects only animal populations in the affected area.

   **D.** It is a sudden disruption that has little effect on plant populations in the affected area.

4. In 1980, Mt. St. Helens erupted. The resulting lahar flowed over a wide area of the Cascade Mountains. Which of these statements best describes the effect of the volcanic eruption? Select all that apply.

   **A.** It affected the living and nonliving components of the ecosystem.

   **B.** It removed populations of mammals from the mountainside.

   **C.** It led to succession on the mountainside.

   **D.** It affected only nonliving components of the ecosystem.

---

**Use the map to answer Questions 5 and 6.**

5. Near the coasts there has been  loss only / loss and gain / gain only  of forests. In north-central Washington and British Columbia, there are large patches of forest loss / forest gain.

6. Historically, the Pacific Northwest region experienced much less deforestation than other regions of the United States. Therefore, populations of organisms living in Pacific Northwest forest ecosystems are likely to have experienced  relatively few / a lot of  changes to their environment. Changes in the populations of tree species would likely  affect / not affect  other populations living in the forest.

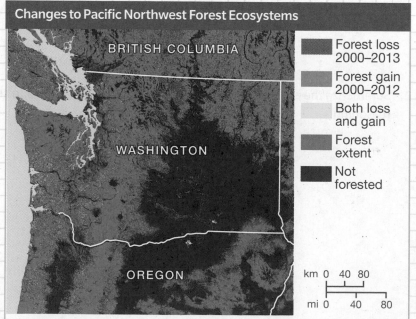

**Changes to Pacific Northwest Forest Ecosystems**

BRITISH COLUMBIA

WASHINGTON

OREGON

km 0  40  80

mi 0  40  80

- Forest loss 2000–2013
- Forest gain 2000–2012
- Both loss and gain
- Forest extent
- Not forested

*Source*: Global Forest Change, University of Maryland Dept. of Geographical Science, 2013.

© Houghton Mifflin Harcourt • Image Credits: ©Steve Davey Photography/Alamy

# Interactive Review

**Complete this section to review the main concepts of the lesson.**

Ecosystems contain populations of living organisms as well as nonliving things.
Ecosystem disturbances change habitats in different ways .

**A.** How do sudden and gradual disturbances affect ecosystems?

Different types of disturbances have different effects on populations. A change in one
part of an ecosystem can affect many populations..

**B.** Use examples to explain how changes to both living and nonliving parts of an ecosystem can affect individuals and populations.

# Maintaining Biodiversity

These solar-powered Supertrees and elevated walkways are in Singapore's Gardens by the Bay. They are inspiring examples of how human creativity can preserve biodiversity.

**By the end of this lesson . . .**

you will be able to evaluate design solutions for maintaining biodiversity and ecosystem services.

# CAN YOU EXPLAIN IT?

## How can biodiversity be maintained in the Everglades without shutting humans out of this endangered ecosystem?

The manatee is just one of the endangered species living in Florida's Everglades, a large wetland ecosystem. Habitat loss and collisions with watercraft are two major threats to manatees.

1. Which design solutions protect biodiversity and consider human needs? Select all that apply.

   A. installing walkways that leave wildlife undisturbed

   B. building houses on a filled-in wetland

   C. using water from lakes to supply farmland

   D. creating fishing and no-fishing zones

2. What ideas do you have for how boaters might enjoy the wetlands of Florida's Everglades without harming manatee habitats?

**EVIDENCE NOTEBOOK** As you explore this lesson, gather evidence to help you explain strategies for maintaining biodiversity in the Everglades.

# Evaluating Biodiversity Loss

As the sun rises on a coastal mangrove forest, all seems quiet and still. But upon closer observation, the forest is full of activity. The forest's network of branches and roots provides enough food for a diverse community of organisms. The underwater roots are a perfect nursery for many fish. The forest is also home to native and migratory birds.

Mangrove forests are full of life. The dense tangle of roots props the trees above high tides.

3. A fishing boat by a mangrove forest spills a chemical deadly to aquatic plants. What changes might happen as a result? Select all that apply.

   A. Many trees become poisoned and die.

   B. Fish eggs fail due to loss of nursery habitat.

   C. Mangrove shrimp become unsafe for humans to eat.

   D. Erosion from the loss of trees causes decreased water quality.

## Humans Rely on Healthy Ecosystems

Humans depend on resources provided by healthy ecosystems. For example, fish breed in mangrove forests. Therefore, the forests provide food and jobs for people who live nearby. The mangroves' dense roots trap sediments and filter out impurities. So, the forests also provide clean water. Mangrove forests even help protect houses near the shore. They block damaging storm winds, reduce soil erosion, and prevent flooding.

The health of an ecosystem, such as a mangrove forest, can be defined by how well it can recover from disturbances. The higher the biodiversity level within an ecosystem, the healthier it is. However, different ecosystems can differ in their biodiversity and still be thought of as "healthy." For example, an arctic ecosystem naturally has far less biodiversity than a coral reef ecosystem does. It is when the biodiversity of an ecosystem decreases from its "healthiest" level that problems can happen. As an ecosystem loses its biodiversity, natural resources become less available. Services provided by ecosystems with lowered biodiversity may also become less reliable.

4. Scientists study factors that help the recovery of coral reefs from damage by boats or pollution. How does this show that science and technology can have positive and negative effects on biodiversity?

Coral reefs have stunning biodiversity. However, they recover very slowly from disturbances because corals grow slowly.

# Ecosystems Provide Natural Resources

Living and nonliving parts of an ecosystem provide humans with natural resources. A *natural resource* is any natural material that is used by humans. Humans rely on ecosystems for natural resources such as fresh water, food, medicines, energy, clothing, and building materials.

For example, few areas on Earth have more natural resources than the Amazon rain forest. The Amazon River flows more than 6,920 kilometers (4,300 miles) across Peru and Brazil to the Atlantic Ocean. It provides water for drinking, transportation, and agriculture. It supports more than 2,500 species of fish and hundreds of species on land. Chemical compounds in rainforest plants are used as medicines. Plants growing in the forests also provide 20% of Earth's atmospheric oxygen. However, there are many threats to the health of the Amazon rain forest. Trees are cleared and rivers are dammed to generate power. The health of any ecosystem affects the health of communities and the supply of resources to them.

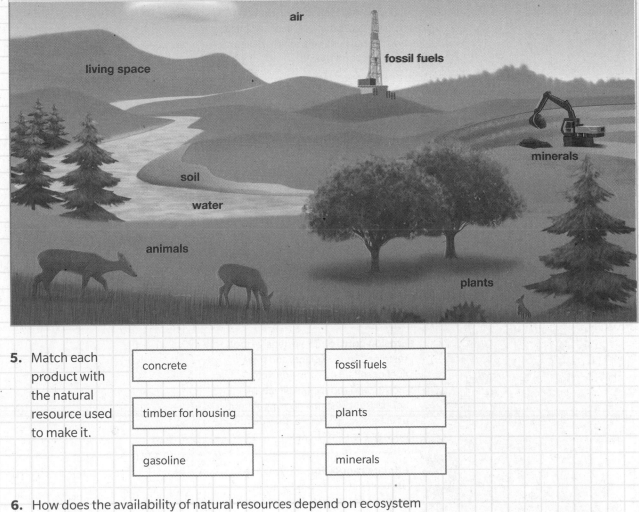

**Natural Resources Provided by Ecosystems**

Humans use or change Earth's many resources to live comfortably.

5. Match each product with the natural resource used to make it.

| | |
|---|---|
| concrete | fossil fuels |
| timber for housing | plants |
| gasoline | minerals |

6. How does the availability of natural resources depend on ecosystem health? Use an example to explain.

# Ecosystems Provide Services

Matter cycles and energy flows through the living and nonliving parts of ecosystems by natural processes. Humans benefit from many of these natural processes. An **ecosystem service** is any ecosystem function that provides benefits to humans. The benefits can be direct or indirect. They may also be small or large. Water purification, nutrient recycling, and climate regulation are ecosystem services. Pollination and pest and disease control are also important services.

## Analyze Threats to Five Ecosystem Services

**7.** What environmental changes might threaten each of these ecosystem services? Include those caused by human activities.

| Ecosystem Service | Potential Threats |
|---|---|
| **Water filtration:** Filtration by soil, rock, and plants provides clean water. Humans use this water for drinking, industry, and recreation. Filtration helps prevent microbe-related illness and the nutrient poisoning of lakes from farmland runoff. | |
| **Decomposition:** Soil microbes break down dead matter and nutrients are released into the ecosystem. This improves soil quality and decreases the need for artificial fertilizers. | |
| **Pollination:** Many plants must be pollinated by animals to produce fruit and seeds. Such plants include over 150 food crops in the United States. Insects and birds are pollinators. They need enough undisturbed nesting sites to live and reproduce. | |
| **Erosion control:** The extensive root systems of native plants and trees anchor soils. Thus, they prevent erosion and reduce the effects of floods. Root systems of crops are not as extensive. Therefore, they do not provide the same benefit. | |
| **Climate regulation:** Tiny marine phytoplankton are producers in marine ecosystems. They carry out more than half of all photosynthesis on Earth. They help maintain levels of oxygen and carbon dioxide in the air and in the oceans. | |

8. **Discuss** What ecosystem services do you depend on every day? Brainstorm ways your life would be different if you did not have these ecosystem services where you live.

## Loss of Biodiversity Impacts Ecosystem Health

When biodiversity declines in an ecosystem, there are fewer natural resources and services to support the remaining organisms. The ecosystem is no longer as healthy, or stable, as before. Biodiversity can decline due to environmental changes such as drought. It can also be reduced by human activities such as urban development and agriculture.

One example of biodiversity loss involves coffee plantations. Coffee plants grow well in the tropical, species-rich areas of the world. There are two main methods of farming coffee. Traditionally, the shrub-like coffee plants are grown in shade. They are planted among existing trees. Leaving the trees standing protects the habitat of birds. The birds eat pests that might damage the crop. The trees drop leaves that cover the ground. This decreases weed growth. It also increases nutrient cycling through decomposition.

Shade-grown coffee plantations protect existing species diversity. The coffee plants produce beans for about 30 years.

As demand for coffee grows, the expansion of coffee plantations into deforested areas is rising. Deforestation removes all plant species from an area. The sun-grown coffee does not get the benefits provided by the trees. So, fertilization is necessary. Cutting down trees also increases erosion and fertilizer runoff into nearby streams and lakes. Sun-grown coffee plants must also be replaced more often than shade-grown plants. Replacing plants is an added cost for farmers.

Humans make choices about how they impact ecosystem health when they get natural resources. Scientists and engineers play an important role in these choices. They research and design ways to maintain biodiversity and ecosystem stability.

Coffee plants grown in the sun produce more beans per acre. But bean quality and volume decrease after about 15 years.

9. In comparison to sun-grown coffee, shade-grown coffee needs more / less fertilization and less / more pesticides. Shade-grown coffee plantations are more / less affected by erosion than sun-grown plantations. The deep root systems of these trees anchor the soil. For these reasons, coffee grown in the shade / sun helps maintain biodiversity and ecosystem health.

# Compare Costs and Benefits of Shade-Grown Coffee

**10.** What is the yearly profit from coffee beans grown in a shade-grown plot and a sun-grown plot?

| Variable measured | Sun-grown coffee | Shade-grown coffee |
|---|---|---|
| Coffee beans produced per plot, per year | 1,600 kg | 550 kg |
| Coffee plants suffering from disease | 5 | <1 |
| Lifespan of plants | 15 years | 30 years |
| Profit per kilogram coffee produced | $2.00 | $2.50* |
| (*Shade-grown coffee sells at a higher price when certified as "bird friendly.") | | |

**11.** Consider the lifespan of the coffee plants. What is the profit at 15 years from coffee beans from a sun-grown plot? What is the profit at 30 years from a shade-grown plot? What type of plot would you operate? Why?

## Main Causes of Biodiversity Loss

Humans love to expand and explore. This leads to important cultural progress, but it also changes ecosystems. Human activities can cause **habitat destruction,** the changing or loss of a natural ecosystem. Habitat destruction removes living spaces and resources needed by organisms.

Most negative impacts on ecosystems are the result of urbanization, farming, industry, or energy production. As the human population grows, resource use also increases. For example, sharks are threatened by overfishing due to the demand for their fins. Shark fin soup is a traditional dish in some cultures. Sharks may also be trapped by fishing nets used to catch other species. As top predators, sharks help maintain biodiversity by controlling the balance of other fish populations. Without proper planning, fishermen may destroy fish populations that provide their source of income. Human activities are the largest threat to biodiversity. Therefore, solutions need to involve changes to these activities.

Humans kill about 100 million sharks every year. To save them, fisheries and consumers of shark products need to be part of the solution.

**EVIDENCE NOTEBOOK**

**12.** Human activities have changed miles of Everglade wetlands for development. How do these changes affect ecosystem health and nearby human communities? Record your evidence.

**13.** Changes in the health of one population can cause a cascade of related effects in other populations. Consider the decline of shark populations. Sharks are predators of sea turtles. Number the phrases in order to complete the cause-and-effect chain.

_____ seagrasses overgrazed

_____ loss of predators

_____ fish nurseries destroyed

_____ sea turtles increase

### Language SmArts
# Evaluate Agricultural Practices

Trees and other plants may be clear-cut to make room for crops farmers grow. This displaces native species and reduces biodiversity in the ecosystem. Reservoir waters used to water crops drain nutrients from the soil. The soil is poor quality and erodes easily. It travels to new locations without adding nutrients to these areas. Fertilizers and pesticides used to maintain crops pollute air, water, and soil.

Farming practices that are environmentally friendly reduce these negative impacts. For example, providing habitat for birds that eat insects helps protect crops without pesticides. Rotating crops helps preserve soil nutrients. Planting cover plants, such as alfalfa, in bare fields reduces erosion, adds nutrients to the soil, and controls weeds.

All native plants are often removed when preparing land to grow crops. The resulting loose soil erodes easily.

**14.** How does the loss of biodiversity caused by changing land for farming affect humans? Circle all that apply.

**A.** decreased air quality as wind draws dust into the air

**B.** increased species diversity in the community

**C.** decreased water quality due to increased erosion

**D.** increased rainwater runoff, which can cause erosion

**15.** Consider this claim: "Removing all native plant life on land for farming is justified because it provides more space for crops. The growing human population needs more products grown by farmers, such as food crops and meat." Do you agree or disagree? Evaluate the claim and provide evidence for your argument.

_____

_____

_____

_____

_____

# Analyzing Strategies for Maintaining Biodiversity

Micronesia is an arc of more than 2,000 islands between Hawaii and the Philippines. Many of the islands are surrounded by coral reefs that are threatened by human activity. Of the 1,400 plant species on the islands, about 360 are found only on the islands. Many of these species are endangered. The islands are remote, so the people of Micronesia depend on the resources provided by the islands. Rising sea levels and human activities are depleting the islands' resources. Activities such as deforestation, overfishing, pollution, and destruction of coral reefs harm wildlife and local economies.

Conservation efforts in Micronesia are underway. They include enacting a multi-island agreement to preserve coastlines, identify coral reefs that need to be protected, and address harmful fishing practices. These efforts show that maintaining biodiversity requires collaboration among scientists, citizens, governments, and businesses.

16. Examine the coral reef photos. How does coral reef bleaching demonstrate how many small changes can weaken entire ecosystems?

Tiny photosynthetic algae live in the tissues of some corals. They provide corals with food and give corals their color.

When populations of the photosynthetic algae inside corals decline, the corals turn white in a process called *bleaching*. The corals lose their main food source. Causes of bleaching include increased water temperature and pollution.

## Protect Individual Species

Officials must choose where to direct limited conservation resources. Protection efforts often focus on species facing local extinction or those that most influence the success of other populations.

One cause of local extinction is overharvesting. This happens when humans reduce the population of a living resource to the point where reproduction rates are too low to restore the population. For example, Pacific bluefin tuna populations have dropped dramatically due to decades of overfishing. Most Pacific bluefin tuna caught are too young to reproduce, which leaves very few reproducing adults. To save the species from extinction, it is being considered for protection under the Endangered Species Act.

Protecting a species is also important if it is a *keystone species*. Keystone species play a vital role in how an ecosystem functions by helping to maintain biodiversity. For example, sea otters are a keystone species that live in the North Pacific Ocean. Sea otters are important to the health and stability of near-shore marine ecosystems because they eat sea urchins and other invertebrates that graze on giant kelp.

**Two Endangered Keystone Species**

*Explore ONLINE!*

Otters are a keystone species. Conservation efforts include protecting them from poachers, nets, and habitat loss.

Conservation efforts for bluefin tuna are failing because governments and fisheries are not working together.

## Protect and Maintain Habitats

Most habitat destruction is the result of land clearing. However, other human activities add to the problems of habitat loss. For example, the Indiana bat must hibernate in cool, humid caves to survive winter. Rising temperatures due to climate change are decreasing the number of caves that bats can use. Also, bothering hibernating bats can cause them to die of starvation. Some 50,000 bats can hibernate in just one cave. So, a single hiker may affect a large percentage of this endangered bat population.

Human activities can also cause **habitat fragmentation**, the division of an ecosystem into smaller areas by roads, housing communities, or other development. Fragmentation makes it difficult for species to have enough space to live. Large predators, such as Florida panthers, often need large land areas to hunt, find mates, and raise young. Without enough living space, these species might face local extinction.

Obstacles that cause habitat fragmentation include roads, factories, housing developments, farms, and recreation areas. Land bridges are one solution to reduce the effects of habitat fragmentation.

## Hands-On Lab
# Model Habitat Fragmentation

You will use sheets of paper to model undisturbed and fragmented habitats. You will compare interior-to-edge ratios to draw conclusions about the effects of habitat fragmentation.

**MATERIALS**
- calculator
- ruler
- scissors
- sheets of paper (2)

## Procedure and Analysis

**STEP 1** Calculate and record the area of each sheet of paper by multiplying the length by the width.

**STEP 2** One sheet of paper will represent an undisturbed habitat. Do not cut this paper. Model fragmentation by cutting the second sheet of paper into 5 to 10 rectangles.

**STEP 3** Measure and record the perimeter of the undisturbed habitat. The perimeter is the distance around the outer edge of the paper.

**STEP 4** Calculate the total perimeter of the fragmented habitat by measuring the perimeter of each piece and adding them. Record the total perimeter.

**STEP 5** The perimeter of a habitat is also called the habitat's edge. Which habitat has more edge?

**STEP 6** If two habitats have the same total area, is more or less edge beneficial to a species? Explain your reasoning.

**STEP 7** **Do the Math** One characteristic of a habitat is its *interior-to-edge ratio*. This ratio is calculated by dividing the area of a habitat by its total perimeter. Calculate the interior-to-edge ratio for each habitat, undisturbed and fragmented.

© Houghton Mifflin Harcourt

**STEP 8** *Edge effects* are the changes to populations that happen at the boundaries between two ecosystems. Edge effects can occur some distance into both ecosystems. Biologists associate a large interior-to-edge ratio with fewer edge effects. Which habitat has the greatest interior-to-edge ratio? What does this mean for the species that live in each habitat?

**STEP 9** On a separate sheet of paper, draw a simple map of an ecosystem. Include human structures (roads, ranches, parks, homes) separated by natural areas (forests, grassland, mountains). Show where you would locate a protected area in the map to limit habitat fragmentation. Would several small, protected areas be as good as or better than one large protected area? Discuss why or why not.

## Prevent Spread of Nonnative Species

In established ecosystems, community interactions between species lead to a dynamic balance of producers, composers, and decomposers. When a new species enters the ecosystem, it can upset this balance. The nonnative species may be able to use resources in the ecosystem better than native species do. By outcompeting native species, they can cause local extinctions of native species. For example, gardeners introduced kudzu vines to the American Southeast. They believed the vine was an excellent ground cover. Farmers also used the vine to reduce soil erosion. The creeping vine grows fast, especially in open areas. It thrives in humid, warm conditions. Once planted, it began to cover existing plants, depriving them of needed sunlight. Scientists now face the difficult task of controlling kudzu growth to protect plant diversity in affected ecosystems.

Kudzu competes with native plants for light and space. It can grow over large structures such as this bulldozer.

## Reduce Pollution

Pollution of soil, air, and water harms many species and their habitats. Chemical pollutants are particularly dangerous because they are usually invisible. They can also travel great distances. Chemicals can build up in the communities they enter. They can build up in the bodies of plants and animals that absorb, ingest, or inhale them.

Some pollution sources include the burning of fossil fuels, fertilizers, pesticides, medicines, and litter. Noise and light produced by humans are also forms of pollution. They disrupt the normal actions of wildlife. For example, the noise from marine oil explorations affects the feeding and mating behaviors of whales.

Pollution can harm species directly and lead to habitat destruction. For example, it can cause contaminated drinking water, acid rain, algae blooms in lakes, and ocean garbage patches.

Under water, plastic bags look like jellyfish. Young sea turtles are at high risk of dying from eating these bags.

# Put Strategies into Action

Reducing habitat loss and pollution requires solutions that involve individuals, businesses, cities, and nations. Scientific studies of these problems can describe their effects. However, the studies cannot identify exactly how society should fix the problems. Society itself must decide on those actions. For example, individuals can help reduce pollution in many ways. They can bike instead of drive and buy environmentally safe products. They can also recycle, reduce litter at home, or volunteer at environmental cleanups. Farmers can reduce pollution by finding ways to grow crops without pesticides. Businesses can reduce waste by using less paper. Cities can reduce pollution by providing low-emission mass transportation. They can also set guidelines for acceptable light and noise levels. Finally, nations can make policies that help reduce pollution, including funding scientific research that focuses on pollution reduction.

## Case Study: Shark Bay Ecosystem

Decreases in shark populations affect many of the ecosystem services provided by ocean communities. Tiger sharks, sea cows, sea turtles, and seagrass live together in Western Australia's Shark Bay. The sharks eat and scare the sea cows and turtles, which in turn, eat the seagrasses. In areas where sharks are less common, sea cows and sea turtles heavily graze seagrasses. Fish and shellfish depend on seagrasses for shelter from predators. Heavy grazing of seagrasses results in less habitat for shellfish. Fish also have fewer sites to lay their eggs and to grow while young. If tiger sharks were overfished and sea cow and sea turtle populations grew too large, seagrass populations would collapse. As a result, fisheries lose profits from declining shellfish and fish populations. The loss of seagrasses also means that fewer ocean plants take up and store carbon. The excess carbon filters back into the atmosphere and contributes to climate change.

The greatest threat to shark populations in Shark Bay and around the world is overfishing. Fisheries capture nearly 100 million sharks each year. This catch rate is unsustainable because sharks can take more than ten years to mature. Females give birth to few offspring and may not give birth some years. So, it takes a long time for shark populations to recover from overfishing. Australian conservation groups identify protecting sharks as a priority. Their efforts include encouraging tourism to Shark Bay, which earns more profits than shark fishing. They are also setting shark fishing limits and creating no-shark fishing zones where shark fishing is banned.

Monitoring the healthy seagrass ecosystem in Shark Bay helps scientists identify ways to help threatened communities. This shark has been fitted with a camera and biosensor. They allow scientists to observe the shark's ecosystem interactions and monitor its behavior.

© Houghton Mifflin Harcourt • Image Credits: ©Micheal Heithaus

17. How does the health of shark populations affect the ecosystem services in the seagrass ecosystem? Select all that apply.

A. Sharks help carbon-capturing seagrasses thrive.

B. Sharks threaten sea cow and dolphin populations.

C. Sharks help protect fish populations for human use.

D. Sharks provide ecotourism opportunities.

18. What evidence in the text about Shark Bay suggests that a reduction in the tiger shark population has a large impact on the populations of other species?

**EVIDENCE NOTEBOOK**

19. Restoration efforts in the Everglades include developing marshes that filter pesticides flowing into the Everglades from farms farther north. How does this strategy directly affect wetland biodiversity and ecosystem services? Record your evidence.

## Analyze the Spread of a Nonnative Species

Humans can accidentally transport species between distant ecosystems. For example, the emerald ash borer is a minor pest of trees in its native habitats in eastern Asia. However, it has destroyed millions of ash trees in the United States. It was first discovered in Michigan in 2002. It is native to Asia and likely came to the United States in wooden shipping crates. Ash tree destruction leaves gaps in forest canopies. Nonnative plants can grow in these brighter-light conditions. Damage to just one tree species may have long-lasting effects on many forest species.

Larvae of the emerald ash borer beetle feed on ash trees. They disrupt water and nutrient transport in the trees.

20. Nonnative species decrease / increase biodiversity by outcompeting native species for resources. They can also upset the balance of an ecosystem by decreasing / increasing the spread of diseases.

21. What are some ideas for technologies that conservationists might use to limit the spread of the emerald ash borer beetle? What might limit the implementation of these technologies?

_____

_____

_____

# Evaluating Solutions for Maintaining Biodiversity

The most successful solutions to biodiversity loss meet the needs of ecosystems and people. They address the need to protect wildlife and ecosystem services. They also allow people to meet their needs and maintain their quality of life. Some of these needs might conflict. Acknowledging and focusing on such needs encourages better collaboration among the many groups that develop and implement solutions.

Creative solutions help meet the needs of both humans and the environment. For example, fresh water is used to produce bottled water, juices, and other beverages. This use of fresh water reduces a limited natural resource. Beverage companies have partnered with conservation groups in watershed-protection efforts. The conservation groups work to restore and protect freshwater supplies using money donated by the beverage companies. Water quality and ecosystems within watersheds benefit from increased conservation efforts. The beverage companies benefit from tax breaks for their donations. They also create a more caring public image for consumers.

## Monitor Biodiversity and Ecosystem Services

Effective solutions begin with understanding all parts of a problem. To understand threats to biodiversity, scientists must monitor changes to wildlife and ecosystem services. Some environmental factors are better indicators of the health of species and services than others. So, this process begins with identifying factors to monitor.

Scientists then evaluate the best ways to gather data. They gather the data and analyze it carefully to identify the causes of decreases in biodiversity and ecosystem services in an area. Scientists conduct research to compare past and present data collected from ecosystems. They look for changes in ecosystem populations, resources, and services.

This scientist gathers data about water quality. The information will be analyzed to determine if conservation efforts are needed.

22. When human activities threaten ecosystem services, why is monitoring needed to design successful solutions? Select all that apply.

A. to determine the severity of the problem

B. to provide data for fundraising efforts

C. to correctly identify causes of declines in ecosystem services

D. to prioritize criteria for conservation efforts

# Define Criteria of the Design Problem

Addressing biodiversity loss or the loss of ecosystem services is challenging. It is particularly difficult when the needs of ecosystems and humans conflict. Ideally, solutions to such conflicts should address human needs and ecosystem needs. For example, in California, nearly 90 percent of floodplain, river, and seasonal wetland habitats have been lost to farming and growing cities. Scientists agree that planting urban forests is a solution to repair lost ecosystem services as urban areas continue to grow. Urban forests also provide shade, improve air quality, control flooding, and raise property values. But urban areas also need wide-open spaces for roads, parking lots, and sports grounds. In this way, the need to plant more trees may conflict with the need of people to go about their day safely.

Volunteers plant trees on a residential street to help increase the number of urban trees in Richmond, California.

There are many possible ways to increase urban tree plantings. The *criteria* are the features of a successful solution. Defining criteria helps to identify the best possible solutions to this problem. Such criteria may include that the trees should be deciduous and native species. Other possible criteria are that the trees or the planting plans should not change current park uses and that falling leaves must not create safety hazards for pedestrians and drivers. Some of these criteria focus on meeting the needs of the ecosystem. Others aim to meet the needs of people. Identifying the solutions that best meet the criteria is the next step in solving the design problem.

# Define Constraints of the Design Problem

Designing effective solutions also requires considering the environmental, economic, scientific, and social factors that affect the solution. These factors help to identify the limitations the solution must work within. They are called *constraints*. Solutions that do not meet all the constraints of the design problem cannot be used. For example, an exciting design solution cannot be used if it is too expensive. One constraint of solutions to the urban forest problem could be that the canopy of mature trees must be less than 30 feet wide to protect road visibility and keep paths safe. Another limit is that established tree species must be able to survive being watered no more than once a week during dry weather since watering restrictions will limit the amount of extra water the trees can get.

**23.** What are some examples of social factors that city planners would need to consider before agreeing on a tree-planting program in an urban area?

**EVIDENCE NOTEBOOK**

**24.** Restoring wetlands involves reclaiming existing ranches and farmland. What are the costs and benefits of this solution for humans and ecosystem services? Record your evidence.

© Houghton Mifflin Harcourt • Image Credits: ©Richard Wong/Alamy

# Case Study: Mountain Meadow Restoration

When trying to maintain biodiversity and ecosystem services, decision makers evaluate how well each proposed solution meets the criteria and constraints of the design problem. This step helps them decide which solution will be the most successful.

Recently, the water levels in California's reservoirs were at historically low levels due to a long drought. Restoring the degraded mountain meadow ecosystems in California's Sierra Nevada watersheds is one proposed solution to help retain water. Meadow plants slow the flow of rainwater and melted snow. Water can then soak into the ground. This prevents flooding and erosion. It also improves the reliability and quality of water flow to streams and reservoirs. It is a long-term drought solution.

However, there are serious barriers to the success of mountain meadow restoration programs. Ranchers living in mountain areas do not support the programs because they reduce available grazing land. Restoration requires many workers, takes many years, and needs long-term monitoring. Also, measuring the positive benefits of meadow restoration is difficult. This makes funding hard to obtain. Government leaders prefer solutions to the water shortage problem that provide immediate, measurable results.

Conservation engineers added a trail above this mountain meadow in Yosemite National Park. The trail helps protect the meadow's plant life from people.

**25.** Mountain meadow restoration is a chosen solution to water shortages in California. Consider each of the criteria listed in the table. Rank the criteria on a scale from 1 to 4, with 4 being the most important. Then explain your reasoning.

| Criteria for Mountain Meadow Restoration Projects in the Sierra Nevada | |
|---|---|
| Criteria | Ranking |
| Increase native species diversity in the restored area | |
| Encourage growth of plants that attract birds and pollinators | |
| Involve volunteer organizations to lower costs and provide workers | |
| Include regular sampling to determine progress and success | |
| Explain your reasoning: | |

# Evaluate Proposed Design Solutions

Once restored, a new mountain meadow could fail. For example, pine trees around the meadow could spread into the area. Pine trees crowd out meadow plants. They increase shade that discourages new growth. There are several solutions to the spread of pine trees into meadows.

One option is to use prescribed burns to remove the trees. Intense fires damage ecosystems by destroying plants and changing soil chemistry. But small fires do little damage, especially if the plants in the fire area are wet.

A second option is to bulldoze pine trees that sprout and remove new saplings each winter. Removing trees on top of snow minimizes the disturbance of soil. This prevents loose soil from being washed away by water. If the soil washes into reservoirs, it would take up the water space and reduce water quality.

There are other possible options to control pine tree growth. Fences could be installed. Native, dense shrubs could be planted to make a physical barrier so that animals could not carry fertilized cones into the meadow.

26. Use the decision matrix to score the proposed solutions to remove pine trees from the meadow. Use the criteria rankings you did earlier to help you score. For example, if you gave a "4" to "increase native species diversity in the restored area," then score each proposed solution on a scale of 0–4. Base the score on how well the solution meets that criterion. For the criterion that scored a "3," proposed solutions will be scored from 0–3. Use this same process for the criteria ranked "2" and "1." When done, total the score for each solution. Identify the most successful one.

| Decision Matrix: Solutions to Reduce the Spread of Pine Trees into Restored Mountain Meadows | | | | | |
|---|---|---|---|---|---|
| Proposed solutions | Increase native species | Encourage birds and pollinators | Involve volunteer organizations | Include regular sampling | Total score |
| 1. Use prescribed burns | | | | | |
| 2. Winter-time tree removal | | | | | |
| 3. Use barbed-wire fencing | | | | | |
| 4. Use native-shrub barrier | | | | | |

27. Think about your top-scoring solution. What are likely cost and social constraints that might need to be met when putting the solution into action?

## Solution Tradeoffs

Sometimes solution priorities conflict with one another. In this case, tradeoffs must be accepted to carry out a solution. For example, a criterion for restoring mountain meadows is to keep cost as low as possible. To meet this criterion, a lot of volunteer help is needed. Volunteers likely lack the experience of experts. So, the project will likely run longer than expected. Therefore, accepting that the project will take longer to complete is a fair tradeoff to reduce costs as much as possible. Another tradeoff might include accepting the increased difficulty and cost of controlling pines in the snow rather than in spring or summer.

Some solutions might no longer work as conditions change. Sometimes, unexpected issues cause the problem to be redefined. Suppose several native shrubs that were moved to the meadow carried a disease. The disease spreads rapidly. Now a new problem needs to be solved to preserve the meadow. New criteria and constraints will need to be identified. Then new solutions can be considered.

Off-road enthusiasts discover a mountain meadow. Restoration plans had to shift to address the new threat to the meadow's health.

## Identify a Solution

Decision makers are choosing a solution to biodiversity loss. They look for projects that maximize benefits and minimize costs. The best solution is often the one that addresses biodiversity loss directly by enacting laws. Solutions may also protect the threatened species or ecological service. For example, overfishing is the primary threat to tiger sharks. A solution that involves an immediate reduction in shark fishing would likely be prioritized over solutions that involve protecting the sharks' breeding areas only.

28. Conservation groups and governments have limited budgets to fund projects. Which of the following solutions is most likely to be chosen to preserve biodiversity?

    A. the one with the fewest constraints

    B. the one that provides the most benefits at the lowest cost

    C. the one that best meets criteria and constraints, regardless of cost

    D. the one that most improves biodiversity

29. Suppose ranchers near a mountain meadow lobby local officials for grazing rights. Their lobbying disrupts plans for meadow conservation. How does this show that science contributes to understanding biodiversity loss and its possible solutions, but it does not dictate decisions that society makes?

    _____

    _____

    _____

    _____

# Continue Your Exploration

Name: _____     Date: _____

**Check out the path below or go online to choose one of the other paths shown.**

| Careers in Science |
|---|

- Hands-On Labs 👋
- Backyard Biodiversity
- Propose Your Own Path

*Go online to choose one of these other paths.*

## Ecotourism

The ecotourism industry tries to provide exciting natural experiences for travelers. Their goal is to preserve habitats and increase awareness of threats to biodiversity. It is a challenge, however, to provide tours to wildlife areas without disrupting protection efforts. Ecotourism companies can maximize benefits to ecosystems by working closely with governments, conservation groups, and citizens to design their programs.

### Case Study: Elephant Conservation in Thailand

Elephants have played an essential role in the industry and culture of Thailand for centuries. Most of these elephants were captured to work in the logging industry. Then, logging was banned. Elephant caretakers (called *mahouts*) began working with their elephants in the entertainment and tourism industries. Not all elephants and mahouts do well in this new work, as care for the elephants is inconsistent and pay for mahouts can be low.

The elephant population in Thailand now includes about 5,000 animals. Only 20% live in the wild. Many elephants live in camps run by conservation groups or by people hoping to earn money by providing interactions with elephants. The camps are popular ecotourism destinations. Yet, some of them focus on tourism more than conservation. Many fail to meet the needs of elephants or mahouts. Ecotourism to those locations may encourage elephant interactions with people that conservationists want to prevent.

Ecotourism activities such as elephant viewing can help conservation efforts when their impact on wildlife is minimized.

185

# Continue Your Exploration

The Elephant Nature Park (ENP) in northern Thailand is an example of how ecotourism can help biodiversity. ENP's mission criteria include being a sanctuary for endangered species, providing rainforest restoration, preserving native culture, and providing visitor education. The park is opposed to elephant shows or rides. It is home to more than 35 elephants and has cared for 200 more, returning them to the wild. ENP is supported financially by visitors, who pay to work at the camp and to care for the elephants.

1. ENP collaborates with conservation groups, Thailand's government, and local monks. The government provides funding and lands. The monks bless trees planted by the park, which discourages illegal logging. What does this tell you about how human culture and conservation efforts influence each other?

2. Inspired by ENP, other elephant camps are changing their ways. They are getting rid of elephant shows to focus on care and conservation. How is this evidence that ENP is meeting its mission criteria?

3. When evaluating the conservation success of the Elephant Nature Park, what additional information would you like to have? Can you rely on the information provided here about elephant conservation in Thailand? Why or why not?

4. **Collaborate** Imagine there is a natural resource in your community that needs protection from heavy tourist traffic. Brainstorm ecotourism-based solutions to this problem. With your group, develop criteria and choose one solution that meets the needs of people and the ecosystem. Present your solution to the class as a brief oral report.

© Houghton Mifflin Harcourt

# Can You Explain It?

Name: _____  Date: _____

**How can biodiversity be maintained in the Everglades without shutting humans out of this endangered ecosystem?**

 **EVIDENCE NOTEBOOK**

Refer to the notes in your Evidence Notebook to help you construct an explanation for how biodiversity can be maintained in the Everglades without shutting humans out of this endangered ecosystem.

1. State your claim. Make sure your claim fully explains how designed solutions can balance the needs of humans with the needs of the ecosystem.

2. Summarize the evidence you have gathered to support your claim and explain your reasoning.

# Checkpoints

**Answer the following questions to check your understanding of the lesson.**

**Use the photo of a banana plantation to answer Question 3.**

3. Banana plantations are planted in tropical forests. They displace other native plants. Bananas are harvested from the same plants year after year. What do banana plantations do in the ecosystem? Select all that apply.

   **A.** decrease biodiversity in the area

   **B.** increase natural resources

   **C.** reduce water pollution

   **D.** impact ecosystem services

4. Undisturbed polar ecosystems naturally have less biodiversity than undisturbed tropical rainforest ecosystems. Which of the following statements are true?

   **A.** Polar ecosystems are less healthy than tropical rainforest ecosystems.

   **B.** Polar ecosystems are home to fewer species than tropical rain forests.

   **C.** As long as they remain undisturbed, both ecosystems are equally "healthy."

   **D.** Polar ecosystems are less important than tropical rain forests.

5. Scientific understanding of biodiversity issues caused by overfishing *can / cannot* describe the consequences of continued overfishing. However, such knowledge *does / does not* identify the decisions society should make.

**Use the photo of a protected habitat to answer Question 6.**

6. Suppose people ignore a sign like this one. What might happen if they walk into the protected area? Select all that apply.

   **A.** increased water pollution due to littering

   **B.** habitat fragmentation from walking trails

   **C.** increased participation in conservation efforts

   **D.** spread of a nonnative species

7. A wetland provides flood control services. Engineers are evaluating competing design solutions to preserve this service. What should they consider?

   **A.** the number of predators in the ecosystem

   **B.** the amount of impermeable ground cover (ground cover that does not soak up precipitation) in the ecosystem

   **C.** the best native plants to plant in the project area

   **D.** the number of pollinators in the project area

# Interactive Review

**Complete this page to review the main concepts of the lesson.**

Humans depend on healthy ecosystems. Biodiversity is directly related to ecosystem health.

**A.** Explain why humans depend on healthy ecosystems for resources and services.

Strategies to maintain biodiversity include protecting habitats and individual species, reducing pollution, and preventing the spread of nonnative species.

**B.** Explain how protecting habitats helps to maintain biodiversity.

Monitoring ecosystems allows scientists to develop solutions to maintain biodiversity and ecosystem services. Choosing the best solution involves evaluating how well each possible solution meets the criteria and constraints of the problem.

**C.** When should conservation groups collect data about ecosystem biodiversity and services?

**Choose one of the activities to explore how this unit connects to other topics.**

## ☐ Engineer It

**Permeable Pavers**  Storm water runoff can lead to flooding and increased water pollution. Water that flows over roads, parking lots, and driveways can pick up pollutants and flow directly into bodies of water, instead of being absorbed into soils. A permeable paver is a solution that has been designed to reduce the amount of storm water runoff.

Identify an area that has an issue with storm water runoff. Research permeable pavers and at least two other design solutions for reducing runoff. Evaluate each solution based on the needs of your chosen area. Based on your analysis, recommend a solution and present your findings.

## ☐ Literature Connection

**Works Inspired by Nature**  Henry Thoreau was a writer and poet who lived from 1817-1862. He wrote about the connection between nature and people. He advocated for every town to have a park or untouched forest. He built a cabin by Walden Pond, near Concord, Massachusetts. His famous book, *Walden,* was inspired by time spent in that cabin.

Research another famous historical environmental writer. Explain what they were advocating for or against. Write a short essay relating their works to modern efforts to protect biodiversity.

## ☐ Technology Connection

**Camera Traps as a Tool in Wildlife Research**  A camera trap is a camera that takes a photo when an animal triggers its infrared sensor. The use of camera traps has provided important data related to wildlife conservation. Examples include evidence that Javan rhinos are breeding, a record of the first wolverine in California since 1922, and evidence that Siamese crocodiles still inhabit Cambodia. Data related to the range and size of populations are important for designing solutions to maintain biodiversity.

Research the benefits and limitations of camera traps. Investigate a case in which data provided by camera traps is being used for the conservation of a species or ecosystem. Create a pamphlet that explains how the information collected by those cameras is helping to maintain biodiversity.

A cougar caught on film by a camera trap in Wyoming.

Name: _____   Date: _____

**Complete this review to check your understanding of the unit.**

**Use the map to answer Questions 1 and 2.**

1. Which part of the United States has the highest biodiversity of reptiles?
   A. Northwest
   B. Northeast
   C. South
   D. Midwest

2. *Purple / Red / Orange* regions on the map would likely be most affected by the removal of one reptile species. In general, areas with *higher / lower* biodiversity remain more stable, recovering *more / less* quickly after a disturbance.

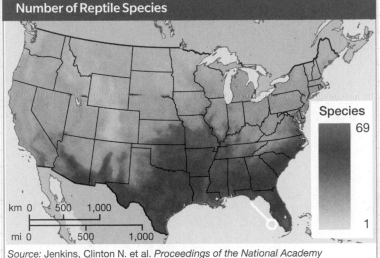

**Number of Reptile Species**

Species
69
1

Source: Jenkins, Clinton N. et al. *Proceedings of the National Academy of Sciences of the United States of America* 112.16 (2015): 5081–5086.

3. *Monoculture* is an agricultural practice of growing genetically similar plants over large areas. Consider an ecosystem change such as a new disease or pest invasion. When comparing a monoculture to a farm field with higher biodiversity, the field with higher biodiversity would likely have *greater / less* risk of massive crop failure due to ecosystem change. A farm field with higher biodiversity would also maintain *higher / lower* levels of soil nutrients over many generations.

**Use this graph of coastal dead zones to answer Questions 4 and 5.**

4. The amount of coastal dead zones *increased / decreased* between 1980 and 2010.

5. Biodiversity in these coastal dead zones is *high / low*. Therefore, the ecosystem health of these areas would be considered *high / low*.

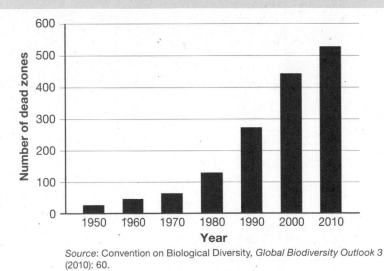

**Coastal Dead Zones Worldwide**

Dead zones are areas in the ocean where the oxygen level in the deep water is so low that most organisms cannot live there. Nutrient pollution is the primary cause of dead zones in the ocean.

Source: Convention on Biological Diversity, *Global Biodiversity Outlook 3* (2010): 60.

6. Complete the table by adding information for each ecosystem type and the impact on that ecosystem.

| Ecosystem Biodiversity | Patterns | Stability and Change | Influences on Society |
|---|---|---|---|
| High Biodiversity | An ecosystem with high biodiversity has a high variety of species, in terms of number of species and genetic variation within each species. Ecosystems with high biodiversity can generally recover relatively quickly from a disturbance. | | |
| Low Biodiversity | | | |

Name: _____          Date: _____

**Use the image of the farm to answer Questions 7-10.**

## Farm Ecosystem

**Plant diversity** A variety of plant species increases the health of soil by providing different nutrients.

**Earthworms** Decomposers return nutrients from nonliving plant and animal matter back to the soil.

**Bacteria** Some bacteria change nitrogen gas into forms of nitrogen that plants can use.

**Mycorrhizae** These fungi help provide plant roots with water and mineral nutrients.

7. Describe the ecosystem services provided by the diverse soil community shown in this farm ecosystem.

8. What might be the impacts on this farm if soil biodiversity decreased?

9. The forested area behind this farm became fragmented when the land was cleared for farming. How might this habitat fragmentation affect biodiversity in the forest?

10. In what ways could biodiversity be maintained on the farm and the surrounding ecosystems?

**Use the image of the mangroves to answer Questions 11–13.**

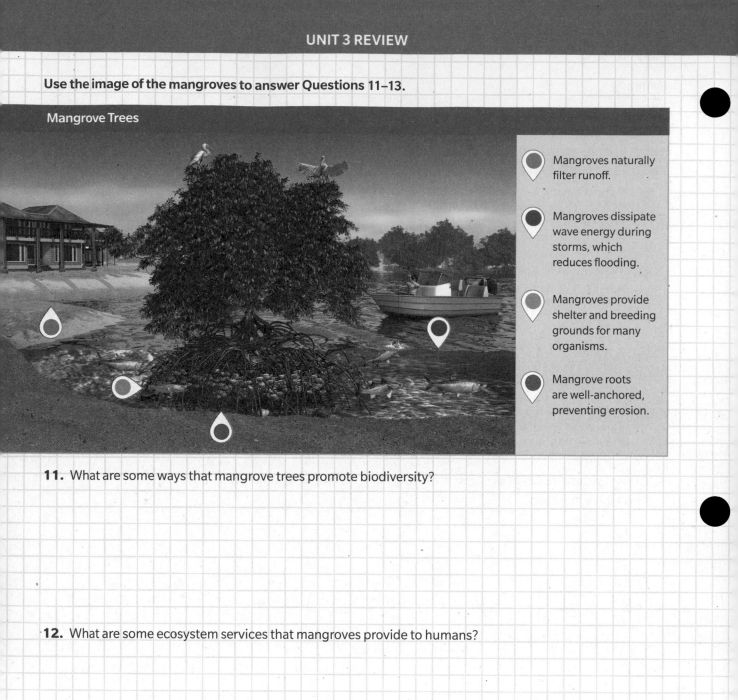

Mangrove Trees

- Mangroves naturally filter runoff.
- Mangroves dissipate wave energy during storms, which reduces flooding.
- Mangroves provide shelter and breeding grounds for many organisms.
- Mangrove roots are well-anchored, preventing erosion.

**11.** What are some ways that mangrove trees promote biodiversity?

**12.** What are some ecosystem services that mangroves provide to humans?

**13.** How would this ecosystem be affected if many of the mangrove trees were removed?

Name: _____     Date: _____

# What is the best way to prevent shoreline erosion?

Humans have developed many solutions to try to prevent shoreline erosion. Compare the shorelines of these two images. In the image on the left, natural vegetation has been maintained along the lake shoreline. In the image on the right, the natural vegetation has been replaced with a stone wall. Research the strengths and weaknesses of each of these solutions, including how each solution might impact biodiversity and ecosystem services. Then make a recommendation to a homeowner on a similar lake who is considering both options. Write a report that highlights your findings.

**The steps below will help guide your research and develop your recommendation.**

### Engineer It

1. **Define the Problem**  Why is it important to prevent shoreline erosion along a lake? Define criteria and constraints of a design solution for preventing shoreline erosion. As you define the problem, consider that the lake is used for swimming, boating, fishing, and watching wildlife.

**Engineer It**

2. **Conduct Research** Compare and contrast the use of natural vegetation and a stone wall for preventing erosion along a shoreline. What are the strengths and weaknesses of each solution?

3. **Construct an Explanation** Explain how each solution would affect the biodiversity and ecosystem services for the lake ecosystem. How might a small change to one component of an ecosystem produce a large change in another component of the ecosystem?

4. **Recommend a Solution** Evaluate each solution based on how well they meet the criteria and constraints. Based on your evaluation, recommend one of these solutions for a homeowner who is considering both options.

5. **Communicate** Write a report that explains your evidence and reasoning for the recommended solution.

✓ **Self-Check**

|  | |
|---|---|
|  | I defined the problem, including identifying criteria and constraints for the design solution. |
|  | I conducted research to learn about two solutions for preventing shoreline erosion — natural vegetation and stone walls. |
|  | I constructed an explanation for how each solution would affect biodiversity and ecosystem services in a lake ecosystem. |
|  | I recommended a solution for a homeowner considering both options. |
|  | I communicated the evidence and reasoning for my recommendation in a report. |

# Glossary

| Pronunciation Key | | | | | | | |
|---|---|---|---|---|---|---|---|
| Sound | Symbol | Example | Respelling | Sound | Symbol | Example | Respelling |
| ă | a | pat | PAT | ŏ | ah | bottle | BAHT'l |
| ā | ay | pay | PAY | ō | oh | toe | TOH |
| âr | air | care | KAIR | ö | aw | caught | KAWT |
| ä | ah | father | FAH•ther | ôr | ohr | roar | ROHR |
| är | ar | argue | AR•gyoo | oi | oy | noisy | NOYZ•ee |
| ch | ch | chase | CHAYS | o͞o | u | book | BUK |
| ě | e | pet | PET | o͞o | oo | boot | BOOT |
| ě (at end of a syllable) | eh | settee lessee | seh•TEE leh•SEE | ou | ow | pound | POWND |
| ěr | ehr | merry | MEHR•ee | s | s | center | SEN•ter |
| ē | ee | beach | BEECH | sh | sh | cache | CASH |
| g | g | gas | GAS | ŭ | uh | flood | FLUHD |
| ĭ | i | pit | PIT | ûr | er | bird | BERD |
| ĭ (at end of a syllable) | ih | guitar | gih•TAR | z | z | xylophone | ZY•luh•fohn |
| ī | y eye (only for a complete syllable) | pie island | PY EYE•luhnd | z | z | bags | BAGZ |
| îr | ir | hear | HIR | zh | zh | decision | dih•SIZH•uhn |
| j | j | germ | JERM | ə | uh | around broken focus | uh•ROWND BROH•kuhn FOH•kuhs |
| k | k | kick | KIK | ər | er | winner | WIN•er |
| ng | ng | thing | THING | th | th | thin they | THIN THAY |
| ngk | ngk | bank | BANGK | w | w | one | WUHN |
| | | | | wh | hw | whether | HWETH•er |

**abiotic factor** (ay·by·AHT·ik FAK·ter)

an environmental factor that is not associated with the activities of living organisms (72)

factor abiótico  un factor ambiental que no está asociado con las actividades de los seres vivos

**biodiversity** (by·oh·dih·VER·sih·tee)

the number and variety of organisms in a given area during a specific period of time (133)

biodiversidad  el número y la variedad de organismos que se encuentran en un área determinada durante un período específico de tiempo

**biotic factor** (by·AHT·ik FAK·ter)

an environmental factor that is associated with or results from the activities of living organisms (72)

factor biótico  un factor ambiental que está asociado con las actividades de los seres vivos o que resulta de ellas

**cellular respiration** (SEL·yuh·luhr res·puh·RAY·shuhn)

the process by which cells use oxygen to produce energy from food (34)

respiración celular  el proceso por medio del cual las células utilizan oxígeno para producir energía a partir de los alimentos

**chemical reaction** (KEM·ih·kuhl ree·AK·shuhn)

the process by which one or more substances change to produce one or more different substances (26)

reacción química  el proceso por medio del cual una o más sustancias cambian para producir una o más sustancias distintas

**community** (kuh·MYOO·nih·tee)

all of the populations of species that live in the same habitat and interact with each other (75)

comunidad  todas las poblaciones de especies que viven en el mismo hábitat e interactúan entre sí

**competition** (kahm·pih·TISH·uhn)

ecological relationship in which two or more organisms depend on the same limited resource (112)

competencia  la relación ecológica en la que dos o más organismos dependen del mismo recurso limitado

**consumer** (kuhn·SOO·mer)

an organism that eats other organisms or organic matter (13)

consumidor  un organismo que se alimenta de otros organismos o de materia orgánica

**decomposer** (dee·kuhm·POH·zer)

an organism that gets energy by breaking down the remains of dead organisms or animal wastes and consuming or absorbing the nutrients (13)

descomponedor  un organismo que, para obtener energía, desintegra los restos de organismos muertos o los desechos de animales y consume o absorbe los nutrientes

**disturbance** (dih·STER·buhns)

in ecology, an event that changes a community by removing or destroying organisms or by altering resource availability (152)

alteración  en ecología, un suceso que cambia a una comunidad al remover o destruir organismos o al alterar la disponibilidad de recursos

**ecosystem** (EE·koh·sis·tuhm)

a community of organisms and their abiotic, or nonliving, environment (70)

ecosistema  una comunidad de organismos y su ambiente abiótico o no vivo

**ecosystem service** (EE·koh·sis·tuhm SER·vis)

a benefit that humans obtain from ecosystems (170)

servicio de ecosistema  beneficio que los seres humanos obtienen de los ecosistemas

**energy** (EN·er·jee)

the ability to cause change (9)

energía  la capacidad de producir un cambio

**energy pyramid** (EN·er·jee PIR·uh·mid)

a triangular diagram that shows an ecosystem's loss of energy, which results as energy passes through the ecosystem's food chain; each row in the pyramid represents a trophic (feeding) level in an ecosystem, and the area of a row represents the energy stored in that trophic level (48)

pirámide de energía  un diagrama con forma de triángulo que muestra la pérdida de energía que ocurre en un ecosistema a medida que la energía pasa a través de la cadena alimenticia del ecosistema; cada hilera de la pirámide representa un nivel trófico (de alimentación) en el ecosistema, y el área de la hilera representa la energía almacenada en ese nivel trófico

**food web** (FOOD WEB)

a diagram that shows the feeding relationships between organisms in an ecosystem (45)

red alimenticia  un diagrama que muestra las relaciones de alimentación entre los organismos de un ecosistema

**habitat destruction** (HAB·ih·tat dih·STRUK·shuhn)

the ruin or alteration of a place inhabited by an ecological community (172)

destrucción de hábitat  ruina o alteración de un lugar habitado por una comunidad ecológica

**habitat fragmentation** (HAB·ih·tat frag·muhn·TAY·shuhn)

the breakup of a continuous area of habitat into several smaller, scattered, and isolated areas (175)

fragmentación de hábitat  división del área ininterrumpida de un hábitat en varias áreas más pequeñas, dispersas y aisladas

**herbivore** (HER·buh·vohr)

an organism that eats only plants (105)

herbívoro  un organismo que sólo come plantas

# M–Z

matter (MAT•er)

anything that has mass and takes up space (6)

materia  cualquier cosa que tiene masa y ocupa un lugar en el espacio

molecule (MAHL•ih•kyool)

a group of atoms that are held together by chemical bonds; a molecule is the smallest unit of a compound that keeps all the properties of that substance (8)

molécula  grupo de átomos unidos por enlaces químicos; una molécula es la unidad más pequeña de un compuesto que mantiene todas las propiedades de dicha sustancia

photosynthesis (foh•toh•SIN•thih•sis)

the process by which plants, algae, and some bacteria use sunlight, carbon dioxide, and water to make food (32)

fotosíntesis  el proceso por medio del cual las plantas, las algas y algunas bacterias utilizan la luz solar, el dióxido de carbono y el agua para producir alimento

population (pahp•yuh•LAY•shuhn)

a group of organisms of the same species that live in a specific geographical area (75)

población  un grupo de organismos de la misma especie que viven en un área geográfica específica

predator (PRED•uh•ter)

an organism that kills and eats all or part of another organism (105)

depredador  un organismo que mata y se alimenta de otro organismo o de parte de él

prey (PRAY)

an organism that is killed and eaten by another organism (105)

presa  un organismo al que otro organismo mata para alimentarse de él

producer (pruh•DOO•ser)

an organism that can make its own food by using energy from its surroundings (12)

productor  un organismo que puede elaborar sus propios alimentos utilizando la energía de su entorno

species (SPEE•sheez)

a group of organisms that are closely related and can mate to produce fertile offspring (75)

especie  un grupo de organismos que tienen un parentesco cercano y que pueden aparearse para producir descendencia fértil

succession (suhk•SESH•uhn)

the replacement of one type of community by another at a single location over a period of time (154)

sucesión  el reemplazo de un tipo de comunidad por otro en un mismo lugar a lo largo de un período de tiempo

symbiosis (sim•bee•OH•sis)

a relationship in which two different organisms live in close association with each other (109)

simbiosis  una relación en la que dos organismos diferentes viven estrechamente asociados uno con el otro

# Index

**Note:** Italic page numbers represent illustrative material, such as figures, tables, margin elements, photographs, and illustrations. Boldface page numbers represent page numbers for definitions.

© Houghton Mifflin Harcourt

© Houghton Mifflin Harcourt

mosquito, 115
moss, 161, *161*
mountain meadow restoration,
182–183, *182*, 184
mudslide, 152
mycorrhizae fungi, *193*

# N

natural eutrophication, 152
natural resources, 169, 189
nitrogen, *7, 7*
nitrogen cycle, 51, *51*, 57
nitrogen fixing, *193*
noise, 177
nonliving environment, 72
nonliving resources
in ecosystem, 44
limited, 92
soil, 86
nonliving things
in coral reefs, 68, *68*
in ecosystems, 132
types of, 86
non-native species, 136, 140, *140*,
155–156
analysis of spread of, 179, *179*
population size control, 114
prevention of spreading of, 177, 189
nucleic acid, 27
nutrient, 12
algal bloom due to, 94
competition for, 112–114
filtration of, 49, *49*
from food, 105
as non-living resource, 92
phytoplankton's use of, 25
recycling of, 170
releasing into ecosystems, 150

# O

ocean
temperature, *115*
vents in, *19*
water evaporation from, 49, *49*

oil drilling, *120*
omnivore, 106
online activities, Explore Online!
5, 21, 26, 32, 43, 52, 55, 85, 99,
139, 150, 175
organelle, 32, *32*
organisms
acquiring matter and energy, 11–16
benefit of commensalism for, 110
cellular respiration in, 34
composition of, 8
consumer, 13
decomposer, 13
energy in, 9–10
energy pyramid of, 48, *48*
matter and energy in, 4–18
needs of, 70, 86–89
organization of, *73*
producer, 12
reintroduction of, 129
osprey, *74*
other elements, 7, *7*
otter, 175, *175*
overfishing, 140, *140*, 172, 174, 178,
*184*
overgrazing, 178
overharvested species, 140–141, *140*
owl, 53, *53*, 129
oxpecker, 124, *124*
oxygen, 7, *7*, 8
in cellular respiration, 34–36, *34*
extraction of energy, 8
living things need of, 34
as non-living resource, 92
production of photosynthesis,
32, *32*
provided by plants, 169
regulation of, 170, *170*

# P

Pacific Northwest Forest Ecosystem,
*164*
Panama disease, 141
panther, 175
parasitism, 111, *111*

parts of an ecosystem
analyzing, 70–72
structure of, 73–78
patterns, 102–116
of biodiversity, 135
effects of competitive interactions,
112–116
feeding relationships, 104–108
in numerical data, 108, *108*
of population growth, 114, *114*
symbiotic relationships, 109–111
People in Science, 53–54, 79–80
periodical cicadas, 94
permeable pavers, 190
pesticides, 173, 177
phosphorus, 7, *7*
photosynthesis, 32, 41
by algae, 105
in carbon cycle, 50
energy from, 9–10, *10*
by phytoplankton, 170, *170*
process of, 32–33, *136*
phototroph, 19
Physical Science Connection
Energy Transformations, 58
phytoplankton, 25, *25*, 39, 170
pine marten, 156
pioneer species, 154
plants
atmospheric oxygen provided by,
169
decomposition of, 5
food source for herbivore, 105
as living resources, 92
matter and energy in, 5, *5*
needs of, 16, 71, *71*
*in* nitrogen cycle, 51
photosynthesis in, 32
of ponds, 44, *44*
as producers, 9–10, *10*, 12
water evaporation from, 49, *49*
water needs of, 86
platypus, 105
Plesiosaur, 6, *6*
poison dart frogs, 78